HIKING WITH NIETZSCHE

HIKING WITH
NIETZSCHE

On Becoming Who You Are

JOHN KAAG

FARRAR, STRAUS AND GIROUX | NEW YORK

Farrar, Straus and Giroux
175 Varick Street, New York 10014

Copyright © 2018 by John Kaag
Map on p. xi copyright © 2018 by Jeffrey L. Ward
All rights reserved
Printed in the United States of America
First edition, 2018

Excerpts from this book originally appeared, in slightly different
form, in *The New York Times* and *Aeon* magazine.

Library of Congress Cataloging-in-Publication Data
Names: Kaag, John J., 1979– author.
Title: Hiking with Nietzsche : on becoming who you are / John Kaag.
Description: First [edition]. | New York : Farrar, Straus, and Giroux, 2018. |
Includes bibliographical references and index.
Identifiers: LCCN 2017057604 | ISBN 9780374170011 (hardcover)
Subjects: LCSH: Nietzsche, Friedrich Wilhelm, 1844–1900. | Spiritual
biography. | Mountaineering—Alps—Miscellanea.
Classification: LCC B3317 .K3195 2018 | DDC 193—dc23
LC record available at https://lccn.loc.gov/2017057604

Designed by Richard Oriolo

Our books may be purchased in bulk for promotional, educational,
or business use. Please contact your local bookseller or the Macmillan
Corporate and Premium Sales Department at 1-800-221-7945, extension
5442, or by e-mail at MacmillanSpecialMarkets@macmillan.com.

www.fsgbooks.com
www.twitter.com/fsgbooks • www.facebook.com/fsgbooks

3 5 7 9 10 8 6 4 2

FRONTISPIECE: Photograph of Friedrich Nietzsche (Time Life Pictures /
The LIFE Picture Collection / Getty Images)

FOR CAROL AND BECCA

Most men, the herd, have never tasted solitude. They leave
father and mother, but only to crawl to a wife and quietly
succumb to new warmth and new ties. They are never
alone, they never commune with themselves.

—Hermann Hesse,
Zarathustra's Return, 1919

CONTENTS

Piz Platta

← to Splügen

St. Moritz

Julier Pass

Silvaplana

Lake Silvaplana

Sils-Maria

Lake Sils

Val Fex

Piz Corvatsch

Maloja

Val Fedoz

0 Miles 3
0 Kilometers 3

Alp Muot Selvas

Piz Bernina

SWITZERLAND

ITALY

to Turin

© 2018 Jeffrey L. Ward

HIKING WITH NIETZSCHE

PROLOGUE:
PARENT MOUNTAINS

Set for yourself goals, high and noble goals, and
perish in pursuit of them! I know of no better life
purpose than to perish in pursuing the great and
the impossible: animae magnae prodigus.

—Friedrich Nietzsche, Notebook, 1873

IT TOOK ME SIX HOURS TO SUMMIT PIZ CORVATSCH. This was Friedrich Nietzsche's mountain. The summer fog that hangs low in the morning had all but disappeared, exposing the foothills a mile below. I came to rest on a well-worn slab of granite and appreciated how far I'd come. For a moment I looked down on Lake Sils, at the shimmering base of Corvatsch, an aquamarine mirror that stretched across the valley and doubled the landscape that was, I thought, already impossibly grand. Then the last of the clouds burned away, and Piz Bernina emerged in the southeast. In fact, I hadn't gone all that far. Bernina, the second-highest point in the Eastern Alps, is Corvatsch's "parent," the culminating point in a ridge that runs north to south, bisecting two massive glacial valleys. After the twenty-eight-year-old Johann Coaz first scaled its peak in 1850, he wrote, "Serious thoughts took hold of us. Greedy eyes surveyed the land up to the distant horizon, and thousands and thousands of mountain peaks surrounded us, rising as rocks from the glittering sea of ice. We stared amazed and awe-struck across this magnificent mountain world."

I was nineteen. Parent mountains had a certain power over me. Looming or distant, the parent is the highest peak in a given range, the point from which all other geological children descend. I had been drawn to the Alps, to the hamlet of Sils-Maria, the Swiss village that Nietzsche called home for much of his intellectual life. For days, I wandered the hills that he'd traversed at the end of the nineteenth century, and then, still trailing Nietzsche, I went in search of a parent. Piz Corvatsch, at 11,320 feet, casts a shadow over its children, the mountains that encircle Sils-Maria. Across the valley: Bernina. Three hundred miles to the west, at the French border of this "magnificent mountain world," stands Bernina's far-removed progenitor, Mont Blanc. After that—absurdly remote, estranged, and omnipresent—rests Everest, nearly twice the size of its French child. Corvatsch, Bernina, Mont Blanc, Everest—the road to the parent is, for most travelers, unbearably long.

Nietzsche was, for most of his life, in search of the highest, routinely bent on mastering the physical and philosophical landscape. "Behold," he gestures, "I teach you the *Übermensch*."

This "Overman," a superhuman ideal, a great height to which an individual could aspire, remains an inspiration for an untold number of readers. For many years I thought the message of the *Übermensch* was clear: *become better, go higher than you presently are.* Free spirit, self-conqueror, nonconformist—Nietzsche's existential hero terrifies and inspires in equal measure. The *Übermensch* stands as a challenge to imagine ourselves otherwise, above the societal conventions and self-imposed constraints that quietly govern modern life. Above the steady, unstoppable march of the everyday. Above the anxiety and depression that accompany our daily pursuits. Above the fear and self-doubt that keep our freedom in check.

Nietzsche's philosophy is sometimes pooh-poohed as juvenile—the product of a megalomaniac that is perhaps well suited to the self-absorption and naïveté of the teenage years but best outgrown by the time one reaches adulthood. And it's true, many readers on the cusp of maturity have been emboldened by this "good European." But there are certain Nietzschean lessons that are lost on the young. Indeed, over the years I've come to think that his writings are actually uniquely fitted for those of us who have begun to crest middle age. At nineteen, on the summit of Corvatsch, I had no idea how dull the world could sometimes be. How easy it would be to remain in the valleys, to be satisfied with mediocrity. Or how difficult it would be to stay alert to life. At thirty-six, I am just now beginning to understand.

Being a responsible adult is, among other things, often to resign oneself to a life that falls radically short of the expectations and potentialities that one had or, indeed, still has. It is to become what one has always hoped to avoid. In midlife, the *Übermensch* is a lingering promise, a hope, that change is still possible. Nietzsche's *Übermensch*—actually his philosophy on the whole—is no mere abstraction. It isn't to be realized from an armchair or the comfort of one's home. One needs to physically rise, stand up, stretch, and set off. This transformation occurs, according to Nietzsche, in a "sudden sentience and prescience of the future, of near adventures, of seas open once more, and aims once more permitted and believed in."

This book is about "aims once more permitted" and sought after, about hiking with Nietzsche into adulthood. When I first summited Corvatsch, I thought that the sole objective of tramping was to get above the clouds into open air, but over the years, as my hair has begun to gray, I've concluded that this cannot possibly be the only point of hiking, or of living. It is true that the higher one climbs, the more one can see, but it is also true that no matter the height, the horizon always bends out of view.

As I've grown older, the message of Nietzsche's *Übermensch* has become more pressing but also more confusing. How high is high enough? What am I supposed to be looking at or, more honestly, searching for? What is the point of this blister on my foot, the pain of self-overcoming? How exactly did I reach this particular mountaintop? Am I supposed to be satisfied with *this* peak? At the doorway of his thirties, Nietzsche suggested, "Let the youthful soul look back on life with the question: what have you truly loved up to now, what has drawn your soul aloft?" In the end, these are the right questions to ask. The project of the *Übermensch*—like aging itself—is not to arrive at any fixed destination or to find some permanent room with a view.

When you hike, you bend into the mountain. Sometimes

you slip and hurtle forward. Sometimes you lose your balance and topple back. This is a story of trying to lean in just the right way, to lean one's present self into something unattained, attainable, yet out of view. Even slipping can be instructive. Something happens not at the top, but along the way. One has the chance, in Nietzsche's words, to "become who you are."

PART I

HOW THE
JOURNEY BEGAN

*He who has attained to only some degree of freedom of
mind cannot feel other than a wanderer on the earth—
though not as a traveler to a final destination:
for this destination does not exist.*

—Friedrich Nietzsche,
Human, All Too Human, 1878

I OFTEN TELL MY STUDENTS THAT PHILOSOPHY SAVED
my life. And it's true. But on that first trip to Sils-Maria—
on my way to Piz Corvatsch—it nearly killed me. It was 1999,
and I was in the process of writing a thesis about genius, insanity, and aesthetic experience in the writings of Nietzsche
and his American contemporary Ralph Waldo Emerson. On
the sheltered brink of my twenties, I'd rarely ventured beyond
the invisible walls of central Pennsylvania, so my adviser pulled

some administrative strings and found a way for me to escape. At the end of my junior year he handed me an unmarked envelope—inside was a check for three thousand dollars. "You should go to Basel," he suggested, probably knowing full well that I wouldn't stay there.

Basel was a turning point, a pivot between Nietzsche's early conventional life as a scholar and his increasingly erratic existence as Europe's philosopher-poet. He had come to the city in 1869 as the youngest tenured faculty member at the University of Basel. In the ensuing years he would write his first book, *The Birth of Tragedy*, in which he argued that the allure of tragedy was its ability to harmonize the two competing urges of being human: the desire for order and the strange but undeniable longing for chaos. When I arrived in Basel, still a teenager, I couldn't help thinking that the first of these drives—an obsessive craving for stability and reason that Nietzsche termed "the Apollonian"—had gotten the better of modern society.

The train station in Basel is a model of Swiss precision—beautiful people in beautiful clothes glide through a grand atrium to meet trains that never fail to run on time. Across the street stands a massive cylindrical skyscraper, home to the Bank for International Settlements (BIS), the most powerful financial institution in the world. I exited the station and ate my breakfast outside the bank as a throng of well-suited Apollos vanished inside on their way to work. "The educated classes," Nietzsche explained, "are being swept along by a hugely contemptible money economy." The prospects for life in modern capitalist society were lucrative but nonetheless bleak: "The world has never been so worldly, never poorer in love and goodness."

According to Nietzsche, love and goodness were not realized in lockstep order but embodied its opposite: Dionysian revelry. His life in Basel was supposed to be happy and well-ordered, the life of the mind and of high society, but upon arriving, he fell into a fast friendship with the Romantic composer Richard Wagner, and that life was quickly brought to an end. He'd come to Basel to teach classical philology, the study of language and original meanings, which seems harmless enough, but Nietzsche, unlike many of his more conservative colleagues, understood how radical this sort of theoretical excavating could be. In *The Birth of Tragedy*, he claims that Western culture, in all of its grand refinement, is built upon a deep and subterranean structure that was laid out ages ago by Dionysus himself. And, in the early years of their friendship, Nietzsche and Wagner aimed to dig it up.

Dionysus did not appear to live in Basel. According to Homer, he was born far from the walls of Western civilization, "near the Egyptian stream." He was the wild child of Greek mythology, the figure that Apollo tried unsuccessfully to keep in check. Also known as Eleutherios—the "liberator"—this rowdy god of wine and mirth is usually depicted as wandering through the hills with his drunken sage of a foster father, the satyr Silenus. Wandering makes it sound more serious than it was; cavorting was more like it—dancing and sexing his way through the trees outside the city limits.

Wagner was thirty years Nietzsche's senior, born in the same year as the philosopher's father, a devout Lutheran who had died of a "softening of the brain" when his son was five. There was nothing soft or dead about the composer. Wagner's middle works were expressions of *Sturm und Drang*—"storm and stress"—and Nietzsche adored them. Wagner and

Nietzsche shared a deep contempt for the rise of bourgeois culture, for the idea that life, at its best, was to be lived easily, blandly, punctually, by the book. "Making a living" was, and still is, simple in Basel: you go to school, get a job, make some money, buy some stuff, go on holiday, get married, have kids, and then you die. Nietzsche and Wagner knew that there was something meaningless about this sort of life.

At the beginning of *The Birth of Tragedy*, Nietzsche recounts the story of King Midas and Silenus. Midas, the famous king with the golden touch, asks Dionysus's companion to explain the meaning of life. Silenus gives the king one look and tells it to him straight: "Oh, wretched ephemeral race . . . why do you compel me to tell you what it would be most expedient for you not to hear? What is best of all is utterly beyond your reach: not to be born, not to be, to be nothing. But the second best for you is—to die soon." As I sat on the steps of the BIS, watching men and women scuttle off to work, I thought that Silenus was probably right: certain types of lives were best lived as quickly as possible. Nietzsche and Wagner believed, however, that being human was to be savored, lived to the fullest.

"It is only as an aesthetic experience," Nietzsche insists in *The Birth of Tragedy*, "that existence and the world are eternally justified." This was Nietzsche's response to the wisdom of Silenus, the only way to overcome modern nihilism. Aesthetic: from the Greek *aisthanesthai*, "to perceive, to sense, to feel." Only in perceiving the world differently, only in feeling deeply could Silenus be satisfied. If agony and death could not be escaped, perhaps instead it was possible to embrace them, even joyfully. Tragedy, according to Nietzsche, had its benefits: it proved that suffering could be more than mere suffering; in its bitter rawness, pain could still be directed, well-ordered, and even beautiful and sublime. In embracing rather than evading tragedy, the ancient Greeks had charted a way to overcome the pessimism that was quickly overtaking modernity.

I was supposed to stay in Basel for several weeks, supposed to spend most of my time in the library, but as I slowly made my way through the city, it struck me that this plan was impossible. The streets were too straight, too quiet, too mundane. I needed to feel something, to break through the anesthesia, to prove to myself that I wasn't just asleep. I was, perhaps for the first time in my life, free to do something other than what I was supposed to do. By the time I got to the university where Nietzsche had once taught, I knew I'd be leaving as soon as possible.

By 1878, the hopefulness of *The Birth of Tragedy* had begun to fade. Nietzsche's health declined as the first signs of mental instability began to emerge. He literally headed for the hills, embarking on ten years of philosophical wandering through alpine terrain—first to Splügen, then to Grindelwald at the foot of the Eiger, on to the San Bernardino Pass, then to Sils-Maria, and finally to the towns of Northern Italy. To take this path was to follow Nietzsche through his most productive period—a decade of feverish writing that would produce many of the seminal works of modern existentialism, ethics, and post-modernism: *Thus Spoke Zarathustra, Beyond Good and Evil, On the Genealogy of Morals, Twilight of the Idols, The Antichrist*, and *Ecce Homo*. On my first and only evening in Basel, I decided that this was the trek I would take—a path that many scholars think charts Nietzsche's ascent of genius and descent into madness.

I woke the next morning before daybreak, went for a long run in order to confirm my suspicion that Basel was utterly soulless, exactly the wrong place for me, and made for the train station. First stop: Splügen, high in the Alps. I thought I might eventually end up in Turin, where Nietzsche would write *The Antichrist* in 1888, shortly before he lost his mind. That was where he'd found something on the edge of insanity: a philosophy meant to terrify rather than instruct us. If we are to read *The Antichrist*, Nietzsche demands that we cultivate "an inclination, born of strength, for questions that no one has the courage for; the courage for the forbidden." Terror has its uses. The questions that scare us the most are precisely the ones that deserve our full and immediate attention. I settled into the thought as best I could. The train eventually left the valley behind—and with it, rather slowly, my fear of the forbidden.

MY FATHER, LIKE NIETZSCHE'S, went crazy when I was four. Nietzsche's died. Mine abandoned his family. My father and namesake, Jan, had been in international banking in the 1980s, specializing in triangular currency arbitrage, a form of trading that exploited currency market inefficiencies between the dollar, the yen, and the pound. Today, computers do the job, but when currency arbitrage first started, men like my father did it. One of my earliest memories is of my grandfather trying to explain what his son-in-law did for a living. He pulled out a box of marbles and showed me three different types: blue, green, and purple. Imagine, he began, that you could trade me ten blue ones for seven green ones. And then you find someone who would trade your seven green ones for twelve purple ones. Now take your purple ones and trade them for *eleven* blue ones. He handed me back the original set of blue marbles, fished another one out of the box, and tossed it to me: "You get that." That's arbitrage—something for nothing, too good to be true.

"What was once done 'for the love of God,'" Nietzsche suggests, "is now done for the love of money." In truth, what was once done "for the love of God," Jan did for the love of money *and* experience. He was an experience junkie: fly-fishing, sailing, driving, riding, skiing, partying, hiking—if you could feel something doing it, he did it. From the outside, he was an obscenely wealthy, good-looking man, with a beautiful wife and two gleaming sons. But appearances are often deceiving. As Nietzsche neared the end of his time at Basel, he confessed, "I am conscious of deep melancholy underlying [my] . . . cheerfulness." My father was conscious of a similar secret, one he tried to mask with a beautiful facade—but it eventually drove him to depression, alcoholism, and an untimely grave. In the end, arbitrage really was too good to be true.

As a child, I had just an inkling about my father's behavior, but at nineteen I was beginning to understand it with the clarity of firsthand experience. Jan felt the lure of what Nietzsche called "the great and the impossible"—a desire to compensate for the sense of having loved and lost something of incomparable value. His own father, who was also largely absent, wasted his life in a stocking mill outside of Reading, Pennsylvania, for a wife who was attracted to money but ashamed of a blue-collar husband who had to actually work to procure it. My grandfather would sneak home in the evening, eat dinner, settle himself in a corner armchair, and pour the sort of drink that makes everything go black. Love was always something contingent, something that had to be earned. And there was never enough. This sense of privation was born not of actual poverty but of a conception of love and affection that is not unique to my family. It is regarded as a deal. Of course, exchanging affections is exactly as fulfilling as exchanging goods and services—which is to say not at all—but this does not keep one from trying, constantly, to trade up. The utter bankruptcy of love's conditions keeps everything in frenetic motion.

After my grandfather died of cirrhosis of the liver, Jan discovered the sort of drinks his father had drunk, and he bought a red leather love seat for the corner of the living room. But mostly he traveled, constantly, always away, in search of the next deal. From one of these trips he just never came back. He ended up first in Philadelphia and then New York. At a certain point I lost track of him.

THE TRAIN PASSED THROUGH Bad Ragaz, on the Liechtenstein border, at the foot of the Pizol Alp. I surveyed the hills above Ragaz, where sheep grazed lazily at the lower elevations. Somewhere among the rocks was the Tamina Gorge, a narrow grotto filled with the healing waters of Pfäfars mineral springs. For seven hundred years pilgrims have made their way up the mountain to restore themselves and wash away the filth of daily life. In the 1840s the water was piped down the hill to fill the now-famous baths of Ragaz. Nietzsche, at the age of thirty-three, exhausted by his years in Basel, retreated to this spa resort in hopes of escaping the migraines that had plagued him since he was a teenager. It was here that he first decided to abandon his obligations as a dutiful professor. "You can guess," he wrote, "how fundamentally melancholy and despondent I am . . . All I ask is some freedom . . . I become outraged at the many, uncountably many, unfreedoms that imprison me." He would leave Basel and turn for higher ground. As Ragaz faded from my view, I could understand the appeal of such a retreat but also the forces that made running away so vexed.

When Nietzsche's father, the pastor, died, the little boy— called "Fritz" for most of his childhood—did what comes naturally to most devout Lutherans: he became even more obedient. In his adolescence he intended to enter the ministry; he was called the "little pastor" by his fellow students— not a term of endearment. Nietzsche was too smart and introspective for his own good, and his classmates teased him mercilessly. If he couldn't be accepted by his peers, Fritz would seek affirmation from God: "All He gives, I will joyfully accept: happiness and unhappiness, poverty and wealth, and boldly look even death in the face, which shall one day unite us all in eternal joy and bliss." The aspiration to joyfully embrace polar opposites, even the starkest—that of life and death—was one that Nietzsche would neither relinquish nor fully realize.

Companionship didn't come easily to the young man, but not because he was rude or self-centered. Quite the opposite. The young Fritz was shy, polite, deferential to a fault. For a long time, his best friends were books. At the age of fifteen—when other teenagers were sowing their first wild oats—young Fritz established an exclusive book club called Germania. There were a handful of members: Nietzsche and a few other boys who were bookish enough to satisfy him. At their inaugural meeting they bought a ninepenny bottle of claret, hiked into the ancient ruins of Schönburg outside Pforta, swore their allegiance to arts and letters, and hurled the bottle over the battlements to sanctify the pact. For the next three years the members of Germania met regularly to share poems, essays, and treatises (this is where a young Nietzsche presented his first philosophical paper, "Fate and History") and to perform Wagner's newest compositions, among them *Tristan and Isolde*. This was Nietzsche's version of fun.

As the train carried me higher, I thought about the absurdity of this sort of childhood—only slightly more absurd than one that included nine-week pilgrimages in homage to long-dead philosophers—about how difficult it was for him to actually fit in.

Fritz attempted to be normal, but things didn't go especially well. When it came to everyday life, he either overdid it or, more often, grew tired of the banality. Upon leaving Pforta, the premier boarding school in Germany, he enrolled in the university at Bonn and made a good showing at being average—drinking buddies, holiday excursions, even a brief romance. He tried drinking like other kids, but on the one evening he truly let loose, he got so thoroughly besotted that he was nearly thrown out of school. Describing the unfortunate bender to his mother, he complained that he "just didn't know how much [booze] I could take." When he joined the Burschenschaft Frankonia, the equivalent of an American fraternity, he reached the limits of his willingness to conform. He actually didn't like beer. He liked pastries. And he liked studying—a lot. When he left Bonn for Leipzig after only ten months, it was with the distinct sense that being normal was a waste of time.

During his late teenage years Fritz had two comforts: his mother, Franziska, and the writings of Ralph Waldo Emerson. He had begun reading Emerson in the early 1860s as he finished school at Pforta, and the American Transcendentalist quickly became, in his words, "a good friend and someone who has cheered me up even in dark times: he possesses so much *skepsis*, so many 'possibilities,' that with him even virtue becomes spiritual." Philosophy at its best was to be learned by rote—not in the sense of mindless memorization, but in the sense of learning something *by heart* and enacting it in experience. This most personal of knowledge was meant to give individuals the courage to determine their own lives, without the guidance of teachers or priests. And then there was Emerson's *skepsis*, the critical doubt that had wedged itself between Nietzsche and the ministry. "There exists in the world a single path along which no one can go except you: whither does it lead? Do not ask," Nietzsche instructs, "go along it." The path of self-reliance would become the high road that would eventually lead him to the Alps.

Nietzsche was drawn to Emerson's Promethean individualism, his suggestion that loneliness was not something to be remedied at all costs but rather a moment of independence to be contemplated and even enjoyed. In fact, isolation, to the extent that it allows one to be free from societal constraint, is the most appropriate condition for a philosopher. This Romantic impulse ran deep with both thinkers; aesthetic experience was life-affirming not in the abstract but in the emotional and intellectual tenor of an individual. At the age of twenty-two, in a letter to his friend Carl von Gersdorff, Nietzsche wrote of his frank admiration for the American: "Sometimes there come those quiet meditative moments in which one stands above one's life with mixed feelings of joy and sadness . . . Emerson so excellently describes them." As he entered adulthood, Nietzsche began to view certain types of experience—these "quiet meditative moments" among others—as a way of escaping the sorrows of life, and he was attracted by the thinker who, in the 1840s, had initiated the experiential turn in philosophy.

It is, admittedly, a strange thought: that one could achieve transcendence by immersing oneself in lived experience, that transcendence was not to be found "out there," but only in a deeper exploration of life. But this idea is precisely what drew young Nietzsche to Emerson. Traditional religious routes to salvation had been cut off in the early decades of the nineteenth century: German "higher criticism," a form of biblical scholarship that read the Gospels as historical documents rather than the word of God, undermined the Church's spiritual and existential authority; contemporary capitalism hit its stride, replacing the cross with the almighty dollar sign; and modern science—epitomized by Darwin's discoveries in the middle of the century—only further eroded religious faith. One could have faith—and experience moments of deep, nearly divine meaning—but only in the tangible, observable flow of existence.

In Emerson's 1844 essay "Experience," published in the year of Nietzsche's birth, he wrote, "No man ever came to an experience which was satiating, but his good is tidings of a better. Onward and onward! In liberated moments, we know that a new picture of life . . . is already possible." This is Emerson at his most hopeful, but Nietzsche understood that Emersonian buoyancy also required one to learn to suffer experience in the right way. For Emerson, self-overcoming was realized in summer moments of joy *and* sadness, the moments at high noon when one realizes that the day is in decline, already half over. This American, a man in his late thirties who had lost his first wife to tuberculosis, was no stranger to personal tragedy, and he would help Fritz overcome, and endure, his own. Published in 1841, Emerson's essay "Compensation," the sister essay to his more famous "Self-Reliance," promised that "every evil to which we do not succumb is a benefactor." Nietzsche spent most of his life trying to internalize this message, echoing it repeatedly, most famously in *The Twilight of the Idols*: "What does not kill me," he asserted, "makes me stronger."

I knew that he had written these words—and the rest of the book—in one insane week of work in Sils-Maria. After exploring Splügen, I would turn there. Maybe I could walk. I'd brought my sneakers and flip-flops. It couldn't be more than twenty-five miles.

ROADS AND RAILWAYS ARE SUPPOSED to connect two points in the shortest possible distance, but in the mountains, roads curve around foothills and bluffs—the only time they're actually straight is in the tunnels, where they pierce the mountain face. I peered down out of the train window. We were getting close to Splügen, and we stopped for a moment at the town of Chur, the regional capital. There was, I imagined, the road that Nietzsche hiked, just a narrow gravel path carved into the granite that disappeared around the next crest. It was splendid. And treacherous. The road had a shoulder of a few feet and a guardrail, and then it dropped off completely for what seemed like a thousand more. The guardrail had been a recent addition. Nietzsche came to the mountains to tread on the edge of the void.

We entered a high valley, higher than most New England mountains, and I came to appreciate, for the first time, the majesty of the Alps. If the beauty of Nietzschean tragedy could be captured in landscape, it was here: quaint, well-ordered Swiss villages dotted a wide, grassy valley floor that slowly, and then suddenly, gave way to walls of rock and ice that met the clouds. Extremes brought together in perfect harmony.

"I ascend the country roads easily," Nietzsche reported during his brief stint in Chur, "everything reposes before me . . . splendid views to my rear, continuously changing, ever-expanding outlooks." Looking around before catching the train to Splügen, I thought that the ascent into the mountains couldn't have been that easy for him. Hiking like this doesn't make much sense—especially to a culture that prides itself on ever more painless ways of getting from here to there. Nietzsche had a word for such a culture: *decadent.* The word comes from the Latin *dēcadēre,* "to fall off"—as in off the rails.

According to Nietzsche and Emerson, modernity had fallen out of rhythm with life. It was out of tune with the basic impulses that once animated human existence. Animals naturally love to play, to race, to climb—to expend energy and relish power. But in our efforts to become civilized and pious, Nietzsche maintained, we moderns had managed to kill or cage the animal within us. With the help of Christianity and capitalism, human animals had been allowed to go soft. When one "went to work," it was rarely for the joy of exercising free will, but rather for the sake of some future paycheck. Life was no longer lived enthusiastically—only deferred.

Nietzsche fled to the mountains for many reasons. He was

sick—suffering from the nausea, headaches, and eye trouble that would plague his later life—and he needed more time for his writing. He was in search of new experiences, deeper and higher. But he was also no longer wholly welcome in Basel. In the philological community the publishing of *The Birth of Tragedy* in 1872 had created a rift between the literalists and the existentialists. The literalists held that the point of studying the origins of language was to "get it right"—to cut through the limits of interpretation in order to grasp the meaning of words as the ancients once understood them. Nietzsche, and a small band of existential philologists, held that this sort of intellectual time travel was both anachronistic and impossible— that the "task of the philologist is that of understanding his own age better by means of the classical world." The point of historical study was to enrich the present moment of experience. This claim was made in an unfinished essay Nietzsche titled "We Philologists" that remained unpublished, at least in part, because of the controversy that already raged around *The Birth*. Upon its publication, Friedrich Ritschl, Nietzsche's longtime mentor and the leader of the literalist tradition, turned on his most promising student.

According to Ritschl, there were two sides to Nietzsche: the brilliant and rigorous scholar who could make sense of the densest and most confusing passages of Greek, and the "fantastic-exaggerated, overly clever" madman "reaching into the incomprehensible." Nietzsche's Dionysian spirit made him few friends in the staid circles of Basel's intellectual elite. The reviews of *The Birth of Tragedy*—one of them by one of his closest friends—were savage. The promising young scholar, who, in the words of one of his famous mentors, "could quite literally do whatever he chooses," was suddenly an academic outcast. So in September 1872 he left for Splügen; it was an experiment in mountain living that he would take up in earnest a few years later. "As we approach Splügen," Nietzsche wrote to his mother, "I was overcome by the desire to remain here . . . This high alpine valley . . . is just what I want. There are pure, strong gusts of air, hills and boulders of all shapes, and, surrounding everything, mighty snow-capped mountains. But what pleases me the most are the splendid highroads over which I walk for hours." When Nietzsche arrived in Splügen, he settled into a small guesthouse at the outskirts of town. If he was equal parts celebrity and pariah in Basel, here he was a stranger, and the villagers treated him as such. Nietzsche wrote to his mother that he enjoyed the freedom of anonymity. "Now I know of a nook," he wrote, "where I can gain strength, work with fresh energy, and live without any company. In this place human beings seem to be like phantoms."

As I disembarked after the five-hour trip, I had to agree: the ephemera of human existence stood in marked contrast to the solidity of this terrain. People slipped out of the train and set off for their tiny houses nestled in the hills. I was left by myself in the station, gasping the thin air, wondering where I would spend the night. But it was only three in the afternoon, and the mountains beckoned. With flip-flops on my feet and a thirty-pound pack on my back, I set off on my first Alpine trek.

I followed an ancient mule track that led out of the center of Splügen into the hills. Small, unassuming signs pointed the way to Isola, a village on the Italian border thirty miles away. I would just go for a short hike and turn back before nightfall. Walking is among the most life-affirming of human activities. It is the way we organize space and orient ourselves to the world at large. It is the living proof that repetition—placing one foot in front of the other—can in fact allow a person to make meaningful progress. It's no coincidence that parents celebrate their child's first steps—the first, and perhaps the greatest, signs of independence.

The trail was relatively flat and even occasionally cobbled, and I covered ground quickly. Walking is practically and physically beneficial, but it has also, for artists and thinkers like Nietzsche, been intimately tied to creation and philosophical thought. Letting one's thoughts wander, thinking on one's feet, arriving at a conclusion—these are no simple figures of speech but reflect a type of mental openness that can be achieved only on the move. In the words of the eighteenth-century philosopher Jean-Jacques Rousseau, "I never do anything but when walking, the countryside is my study." The history of philosophy is largely the history of thought in transit. Of course, many philosophers came to rest in order to write, but this was, at most, a perching, a way to faintly mark the ground that had been covered. The Buddha, Socrates, Aristotle, the Stoics, Jesus, Kant, Rousseau, Thoreau—these thinkers were never still for very long. And some of them, the truly obsessive walkers, realized that wandering can eventually lead elsewhere: to the genuine hike. This is the discovery that Nietzsche made in the Alps.

At the age of thirty, he was still strong enough to dream of the ascent: "To climb as high as any thinker has ever climbed, into the pure icy Alpine air, where no fog rises to veil things over and where the general constitution of things expresses itself in a rough and lapidary fashion, but with the greatest intelligibility!" Hiking, unlike most vocations, is work with its own immediate reward, and its unpleasant aspects are often the most advantageous. The dull ache of lactic acid building in your quads and calves slowly reminds you that flesh—*your* flesh—is still alive. The control that one has over the pain is strangely affirming: Can you make it to the next rise, to the next outcropping of rocks? Life is often painful or bothersome, but the hiker, at the very least, gets to determine how he or she is meant to suffer.

Four miles into my "hike" to Isola, I slipped out of my sweaty flip-flops, toppled backward, and tore most of the skin off my heel. Hobbling back to Splügen, I snuck into a barn on the outskirts, spread out my sleeping mat, and bedded down for the night. I'd have to patch myself up and resume my search for the Antichrist tomorrow. For Nietzsche, I consoled myself, the point was not about avoiding or even conquering suffering: he recognized, like so many philosophers before him, that suffering was a fundamental fact of human existence. But the ascetic response to suffering was to understand it as a complaint about life. My challenge—the challenge Nietzsche raises—was to embrace life with all its suffering. When he wrote, at the very end of his career, "Have I been understood? Dionysus versus the Crucified," he meant to show that suffering does not refute life as we experience it but must be welcomed, embraced, in exactly the same way we welcome and embrace happiness. In fact, Nietzsche often sounds as though happiness is at best a kind of secondary goal. In *Thus Spoke Zarathustra*, Nietzsche's most famous character, having spent his life in the mountains, concludes: "Happiness? Why should I strive for happiness? I strive for my work."

I spent two weeks in the hills around Splügen, acquainting myself with the joys of moving and the discomfort of standing still. The days were glorious, and they flew by. The nights lasted forever. Boredom, stiffness, sunburn—as soon as I stopped walking, everything caught up to me. I should have been exhausted, but I wasn't. All I wanted was for the sun to rise so that I could be off again. "All truly great thoughts," Nietzsche informs his reader in *The Twilight of the Idols*, "are conceived while walking." To a young philosophy student, the simple correlate followed: the more walking the better. Most of the demanding trails through the Alps aren't really trails at all. Just faint whispers marked by scuffs in the earth and misplaced stones. Here it is possible to realize the hidden essence of walking—that where to go, and how to get there, is entirely up to you. "Each soul," Emerson wrote in his lecture "Natural History of the Intellect," "walking in its own path walks firmly, and to the astonishment of all other souls, who see not its path." There is a fearful liberty in this, and it is, as I found out, difficult to keep one's footing. But once you begin to hike, it is extremely hard to ever fully come to rest.

IN HINDSIGHT, I KNOW I should have been more terrified of the mountains. Instead, after days of hiking around Splügen, I tried to conquer them. As the crow flies, Sils-Maria, the small village where Nietzsche wrote *Thus Spoke Zarathustra*, was only thirty-one miles away. But crows don't fly between Splügen and Sils-Maria. They go *around* Piz Platta, the highest point in the Oberhalbstein Alps. At 11,129 feet, the mountain can be seen on a clear day from a plane flying two hundred miles away, but as you enter the foothills of the Alps, the truly monstrous peaks are obscured by merely sublime ones. I purchased a light coat, a headlamp, and a walking stick, which I thought would be more than sufficient to get me there. Just to be safe, I bought a compass and a map to keep me pointed in the right direction—I planned to blaze a shortcut through the mountains—and a sleeping bag in case it got a little cold. Then I walked, scrambled, and climbed for fifteen hours, straight toward Platta, straight into the darkness.

I'd never camped in the backcountry before. The sun sank behind the peaks to the west, and the temperature dropped. The night would be, I could already tell, more than a little cold. Why hadn't I stayed on the goddamn mule track? Quickening my pace, I looked for some semblance of shelter, but high above the tree line, shelter is woefully scarce. In the end, I found a depression in the granite face—calling it "a cave" would be an exaggeration—and bedded down for the night. Darkness descended. I'd brought matches but forgotten to gather wood along the way.

Calm down: there was nothing to be afraid of. I'd not seen another human being since I'd cut off the path in the morning. This meant that no one would find my body, but it also meant that no one would kill me in the night. Plus, the Swiss are not a murderous people. There was nothing to be afraid of. The only sign of life had been the occasional marmot and the intermittent sound of cowbells far below. There were maybe a hundred lynx in the Alps, and more than enough sheep in the valleys to keep them sated. The wolves and bears, I thought, had been wiped out decades ago. There was nothing to be afraid of. A few stars kept me temporary company but then vanished behind clouds that blanketed the mountains. I was finally, as I'd often suspected, perfectly alone.

There it was: utter blackness—the "nothing" that I was afraid of. In the beginning, according to Nietzsche, man "was surrounded by a fearful void—he did not know how to justify, to account for, to affirm himself; he suffered from the problem of his meaning." I turned my headlamp on and shined it full power into the night. The beam stretched out, dissipated, and vanished. "Once upon a time," Nietzsche writes in *On Truth and Lies*, "in some out of the way corner of the universe . . . there was a star upon which clever beasts invented knowing . . . After nature had drawn a few breaths, the star cooled and congealed, and the clever beasts had to die." To work so hard, to burn so bright, and then to be snuffed out without warning or explanation—this was the idea that haunted Nietzsche as he set off into the Alps.

I bore down inside the sleeping bag, but my ears and face throbbed as the wind picked up. When the morning arrived, I was still awake. I barely remember how I got back to Splügen, but I know it took me two solid days. Frostnip or windburn left a scar on my earlobe—it remains, until very recently the only sign that I'd actually made the mad trip.

AFTER THAT NIGHT, nothing frightened me, and I longed for depth and height. A week later I walked and hitchhiked the fifty—not thirty-one—passable miles from Splügen to Sils-Maria and took up residence at the Nietzsche-Haus, the boardinghouse where Nietzsche summered in the 1880s. It is nestled in an outgrowth of ancient fir at the base of a foothill. Nietzsche's *Thus Spoke Zarathustra* is the story of a mountain man. "Having attained the age of thirty," the narrator explains, "Zarathustra left his home and the lake of his home and went into the mountains." But by the time Nietzsche wrote these lines, he'd flirted with, and nearly succumbed to, the danger of absolute isolation. Zarathustra is a hermit, true enough, but he also secretly craves companionship. As the chapters unfold, he shuttles between the wild solitude of the high caves and the ordered life of the towns below. The point was not permanent escape, but rather to get a breath of fresh air on the peaks in order to be alive among his companions in the towns on the valley floor. This was no simple task, as it meant preserving individualism in the midst of society, interacting with others without being absorbed by the group.

Of course, at the age of nineteen, I had no idea how to manage such a feat, opting instead for solitude and the void.

Today, the first floor of the Nietzsche-Haus is a museum, a mix of contemporary art and Nietzschean artifacts: his original death mask, photographs, and letters written during his stay. Above the museum are three bedrooms that can be rented by the scholars and artists who come to Sils-Maria for inspiration. A small scholarly workshop on Nietzsche and the paintings of Gerhard Richter had ended, and the attendants vacated the Haus, so I was given my choice of rooms. Obviously I picked the one closest to Nietzsche's—a raw-paneled bedroom with a single bed, a desk, and a lonely table lamp. When the sun set, the entire house, save for that lamp, slowly went dark. I spent the early evenings in the halls of the Nietzsche-Haus, contemplating the Richters that had been left behind on the walls: shimmering photos of skulls overlaid with splatters of paint. "Perish in pursuing the great and the impossible": the words haunted these pictures. The painter had followed Nietzsche in making Sils his home away from home, and this is what he'd found.

Thirty-one days dilated, compressed, and slipped away. I stopped eating and sleeping. My hair grew shaggy and my pants loose. My mother, on the one occasion that I called her, observed that I sounded a "little off," which is the Calvinist way of saying "completely insane." She wasn't entirely wrong. Living with Nietzsche can have this effect. When you starve or overwork a body, it will eventually die, but before that, the adrenal glands give off one last burst of superhuman energy in a final attempt to stay alive. In my last week in Sils-Maria, I came as close as I ever have to understanding Nietzsche's claim, "I am no man. I am dynamite!" Evening after evening, wide-awake, no longer even hungry, I returned to my desk, to my *Zarathustra*. At the first sign of light I'd make my way to the trails behind the Haus and do my best to embody him.

At one point in this philosophical poem, Zarathustra asks Life: *"Ich bin der Jäger: willst du mein Hund, oder meine Gemse sein?"* "I am the hunter: will you be my hound or will you be my kill?" This is a question I could never answer. *Gemse* is often understood as "kill," but the more literal translation is "chamois": strange, elusive animals, mountain goats that I imagined still dwelled in the high country above Sils-Maria, subsisting on the spare, almost nonexistent vegetation above the tree line. They were strong and solitary and sure-footed. In the fall of 1888, during his last visit to Sils-Maria, Nietzsche was awakened in the predawn as his landlord slipped out to hunt them in the shadowy hills. At the time, reflecting on the writing of *Twilight of the Idols*, one of his darkest, most enigmatic books, Nietzsche admitted, "Who knows! Perhaps I too was out hunting chamois."

I did my best to continue the hunt and searched in vain for these Pan-like creatures: reading at night, scrambling toward the cliffs during daylight. Half of me was drawn to the radiant peaks, to the mirrored sunlight that graced the surrounding hills, but as the days passed, I began to feel, first faintly and then with growing force, a fascination with the depths that can be found only in the mountains. Some of the most dramatic summits, I learned, are the best places to view the gorges and chasms of life. Exploring Nietzsche's life—vibrant and productive—is also to confront his recurring desire to escape it. He lived in the face of a persistent temptation to die. "It is not in our hands," Nietzsche writes in *The Twilight of the Idols*, "to prevent our birth but we can correct this mistake . . . the man who does away with himself performs the most estimable of deeds." There is, indeed, something respectable about doing away with oneself, about taking control of time's evanescence. I was terrified of slipping away unconsciously, departing before I knew it.

To fast is to regulate life, to put it on a short leash, to do away with oneself slowly with premeditated accuracy. It is protracted suicide. At some point in the lingering days of August, a month before my twentieth birthday, I decided my fast was taking too long. In the rocks behind Nietzsche's summerhouse I laid my plans. I could intensify the fast, but that would, I already knew, have unforeseen effects. I'd pass out, and some good Samaritan would take me to the hospital, where other good Samaritans would pump me full of IV fluids and discharge me with the thoughtful suggestion to "take it easy." Pills would work better, but I didn't have any. Buying a gun in Switzerland was not an option for an American kid. Slitting my wrists seemed self-indulgent and melodramatic, like something a real teenager would do. I'd seen a nylon rope in the first-floor closet of the Haus. Gasoline and a match, maybe. All of it seemed incredibly clichéd, but also more than theoretically possible. For a surprising number of people, the most frightening part of suicide is the idea of not succeeding. The outcome seems preferable to life, but the deed is difficult and very risky. When I summited Corvatsch, I'd seen a crevasse that would probably suffice, but the "probably" continued to worry me. Nietzsche contemplated this sort of nothingness during his stay in the Alps. As he wrote his *Zarathustra*, he measured one's strength by the willingness to stand face-to-face with these forbidden possibilities: "He who seeth the abyss, but with eagle eyes, he who with eagle's talons graspeth the abyss: he hath courage." These are Zarathustra's words—hopeful, brimming with power—not Nietzsche's. Nietzsche would be steadfast, but also more vulnerable, more human, on the brink of these dangers. In the New Testament, the void is described as the place where monsters and demons live; by the thirteenth century, Christian mystics began to conceive of the abyss as the mystery of the sublime Godhead. Whatever it is—demon or God—it is waiting for you. Nietzsche insists that "if thou gaze long into the abyss, the abyss will also gaze into thee."

The chasm on Corvatsch was narrow, six feet wide, and maybe two hundred and fifty feet to the bottom. In my last days there, I slept outside, next to a giant boulder on the glacial plain in the Val Fex. And I visited my abyss often, pitching stones over the edge, sounding the depths, trying to calculate the exact height by how long the rocks took to smash against the boulders below. One hundred feet? Two hundred? I could never figure it out. If I went headfirst, it would work, or I would break my spine and never walk again. More likely, I'd succeed—but not in the way I intended—by bleeding out slowly. Self-inflicted pain was one thing, but dying in some botched attempt seemed to defeat the purpose. So I waited. Yet the idea was always still there when I awoke.

Obviously, perhaps luckily, I chickened out. On what was supposed to be my last evening in Sils-Maria, I broke down and ate. I made my way up a small rise behind the Nietzsche-Haus to a hulking hotel that continues to strike me as one of the grandest buildings I've ever entered. I had six hundred dollars left—a largesse born of Spartan living—and I spent more than half of it at dinner. The courses—all six of them—were minuscule. But they added up, over the course of three hours, to a great deal. So did the small glasses of wine that continued to appear and numb my sense of guilt and embarrassment. At the end of the night I succeeded in exiting the grand foyer without tripping or vomiting. I'm not exactly sure how. And back at the Nietzsche-Haus, tucked into its now warm and inviting privacy, I finally slept. And slept and slept—it was almost noon when I awoke. I'd missed my bus to Turin, but on some level I was relieved. "Companions, I need," Zarathustra admitted, "and living ones—not dead companions or corpses I carry wherever I go. But living companions I need who follow me because they wish to follow themselves—and to the places whither I wish to go." Perhaps I'd go to Turin next time. And next time, I wouldn't come alone.

ENDURING COMPANIONS

*A man's maturity—consists in having found again the
seriousness one had as a child, at play.*

—Friedrich Nietzsche,
Beyond Good and Evil, 1886

"PAPA, WHAT HAPPENED TO YOUR EAR?"
It was seventeen years later, and I was in the home-
stretch of bathing our three-year-old daughter. She'd recently
become obsessed with bruises, scrapes, and scars—artifacts of
bygone wounds—and the mark on my ear had faded but obviously not completely disappeared. Two wet hands grabbed my
neck and pulled my face down to eye level. With her mouth

an inch from my cheek, a closeness that made evading her question impossible, Becca slowly, deliberately, repeated herself: "Papa, what *happened?*"

No one had ever asked me, and I, for so many reasons, had never brought it up. In *Zarathustra*, Nietzsche explains that a child gives voice to a "sacred Yes," a rare moment of permission in the restrictiveness of adult life. For a child, there is no such thing as a forbidden question. So I answered as honestly and expeditiously as possible: Papa had gone on a hike, to a place called Switzerland; one night he slept on a mountain, and his ear had gotten very, very cold. Of course she wanted to know why her father hadn't taken a blanket or a hat, and I was about to explain when Carol, Becca's mother, stuck her head into the bathroom and saved me from permanently scarring our toddler. "That's an interesting story, Papa," Carol remarked. "Why don't you tell a *different* one." Wrapping Becca in a towel, I trundled her off to the nursery, but as I passed Carol in the hallway, she gave me permission to return to a memory I'd often avoided: "Sounds like quite the trip," she whispered. "We should go back."

I had found companions and finally reached parenthood. It was, as it is for many philosophers, an arduous trek: through a ten-year relationship that ended in divorce, through what most of my family and friends took as a scandalously sudden remarriage, all the way to a delivery room at Mass General Hospital, where I met a small, helpless stranger who became our most intimate companion. And now to the nursery and a choice that led me back to the childless Nietzsche.

AT CAROL'S SUGGESTION, I taught a seminar on Nietzsche that spring, burying myself and my students in his texts. It had been years since I'd read these books, and my colleagues were surprised that I wanted to teach the class, but what I really wanted was to think through what a summer in the Alps might mean. Carol joked that it was a good thing that I was a humanist and not a social scientist, as the class would never get past the IRB—the institutional review board that protects human participants in research studies. It was, I had to admit, somewhat brutal. "I profit from a philosopher only insofar as he can be an example." If Nietzsche is right about this, how can we profit from him? How can *he* be our example? That is the question I posed at the beginning of class.

"I used to be happy," one of my students informed me halfway through the term, "then I started reading Nietzsche."

But we kept reading, and for the first time in my nine years of teaching not a single student dropped the class. Most of the students were just shy of twenty, so we started there: Nietzsche became a young man in Leipzig, in what today would be regarded as graduate school. "The amount of work my brother succeeded in accomplishing during his student days," his sister, Elisabeth, recounted, "really seems almost incredible." Here he began his career as a philologist with a reading of *Lives of Eminent Philosophers* by the Greek historian Diogenes Laertius. When Nietzsche graduated, he submitted his prizewinning thesis on the topic, with an epigraph from Pindar that would serve as the cornerstone of his life's work: "Become who you are."

During his time in Leipzig, Elisabeth described her brother, who would later suffer from incapacitating migraines, as a "bear" who "did not know what headaches or indigestion meant." Bears are robust—but also solitary—creatures, and Nietzsche spent his final days as a university student perfecting the art of being alone. He wrote in his journal that he wandered through the streets of Leipzig lost in thoughts that shuttled between anxiety and depression. On one of these trips he came across the work of Arthur Schopenhauer. "I happened to be near the shop of Rohne, a second-hand book-seller," Nietzsche reported, "and I took up the *World as Will and Idea* . . . I do not know what demon suggested that I take the book home with me." But he took the suggestion and "gave [himself] over to that gloomy genius." Becoming who you are meant, at least at first, becoming deeply depressed.

Over the years, I'd conveniently forgotten Nietzsche's obsession with Schopenhauer, the "gloomy genius," the son of a wealthy businessman and a beautiful mother who were happy enough to raise their children in the *haute bourgeoisie*. When Arthur was a child, his family traveled widely, particularly to England and France, for business and pleasure. His father, however, despite being extremely successful, was never truly happy. He fell—or, more likely, jumped—to his death when Arthur was seventeen. I began to remember why I had forgotten.

As Nietzsche came to understand, the loss of a parent vibrates through the life of a child. At first Schopenhauer committed himself to the life of commerce and trade as a way of preserving, or at least honoring, his father's legacy. If Nietzsche was the "little pastor," the teenage Schopenhauer was the "little capitalist." But after two years Arthur grew weary of the family business, discovering that the acquisition of wealth couldn't fill the existential vacuum that opened after his parent's abrupt departure. Schopenhauer's mood darkened; his emotional swings became, and remained, more severe. He could have easily followed his parent to the grave, but instead he, like Nietzsche, like many fatherless sons, decided to dedicate himself to the fathers of philosophy. He had inherited no small amount of money, which he invested shrewdly; his family's worldly fortune, ultimately, allowed Schopenhauer to become a thinker.

I'd often thought that philosophy had a paradoxical effect on Nietzsche and Schopenhauer: it allowed them to come to terms with life, but it made living with others nearly impossible. The pessimism they developed in the middle of the nineteenth century stemmed from the belief they'd acquired in boyhood that human existence is unavoidably wicked. They refused to deny or gloss over the suffering of the world. If there was any meaning to life, it had to be found *in* suffering. In 1850 Schopenhauer wrote: "Unless *suffering* is the direct and immediate object of life, our existence must entirely fail of its aim. It is absurd to look upon the enormous amount of pain that abounds everywhere in the world, and originates in needs and necessities inseparable from life itself, as serving no purpose at all and the result of mere chance." Either suffering is the meaning of life, or there is no meaning of life.

Perhaps this sounds overly bleak, but Nietzsche, echoing Schopenhauer, believed that the ways in which most individuals sought to alleviate agony only deepened it in the end. Typical escapes—food, money, power, sex—are painfully transitory. Life goes only one way, into ever-steeper decline. This is true for all living beings, but humans have the unique powers of recollection and foresight, so they, unlike mere beasts, can relive the horrors of life and clearly envision their untimely demise.

Of course, one can find distractions—politics, education, religion, and family life—but these do little to mitigate the painful effects of being human. These relationships and institutions are as fragile and unreliable as the lives that support them.

Schopenhauer's philosophical pessimism struck his mother, Johanna, as wholly out of sync with life, or at least with hers. He was as difficult personally as he was philosophically, prone to long spells of depression and sudden fits of rage. He paid damages for twenty years to a woman he'd physically assaulted (she was talking too loudly outside his door). When Schopenhauer was twenty-six, Johanna wrote to her son, informing him of the obvious—he was impossible. She described the negative effects he had on his companions, suggesting that he move far away from her. He did. They never saw each other again. She died twenty-four years later. After being estranged from his second parent, Schopenhauer spent the remaining forty-six years of his life alone, cultivating a reputation as the Continent's bachelor-turned-hermit. This is not to suggest that he was a complete stranger to love. He entered an intense, fluctuating affair with the singer Caroline Richter, but given her many suitors and Schopenhauer's perennial (and understandable?) insecurities about lasting intimacy, it is not surprising that it never bloomed into a long-term relationship. "Marrying," Schopenhauer tells us, "means to grasp blindfolded into a sack hoping to find an eel amongst an assembly of snakes."

NIETZSCHE SAW SOMETHING IN SCHOPENHAUER: himself. "From every line I heard the cry of renunciation, denial, and resignation," he wrote of Schopenhauer's writing; "I saw in the book a mirror in which the world, life itself, and my own soul were all reflected with horrifying fidelity." As the rest of the reading club Germania's boys came of age and got married, Nietzsche remained alone in Leipzig and then in Basel, wedded only to his work. At the high mark of their friendship, Richard Wagner traced Nietzsche's mental imbalance to a single root cause: "There seems to be a lack of young women" in your life, the composer observed. This wasn't entirely true, but Nietzsche, while remaining on the lookout for a suitable partner, had yet to find one.

There are certain things that I did not share with my students—such as how Nietzsche's difficulties in love are endemic to the discipline of philosophy. My first wife and I met in college, in a seminar on European existentialism, at the height of my Nietzschean craze. She was writing her thesis on the Danish philosopher Søren Kierkegaard and his method of "indirect communication." This is a maddeningly subtle maneuver, an intellectual sleight of hand perfected by Socrates in which a message is expressed in such a way that an author can sidestep responsibility for making the claim (this is why so many of Kierkegaard's books are pseudonymously written). This is supposed to have some profound pedagogical function whereby a teacher can teach without becoming an idol and a student can learn without becoming a follower. In theory, this sounded almost Nietzschean—and in hindsight, I know it is—but at the time, I regarded it as a mixture of passive aggression and bad faith that ran counter to existential freedom. She and I fought as only philosophers can: incessantly, intimately, bordering on erotic passion. And this is what carried us into marriage.

When it came to romance, Kierkegaard had only slightly better luck than Nietzsche. The Dane was engaged to a beautiful and intelligent woman, Regine Olson, but as their marriage approached, Kierkegaard had second thoughts and decided that his melancholy made him unsuited to a long-term union. My wife and I should have come to that decision. Instead, we were married in a little church in central Pennsylvania. At some point in the early years of our marriage, probably owing to sheer exhaustion, we both stopped reading our existentialists and began to study academic subjects that were more amenable to psychological and interpersonal health. She turned from Kierkegaard to a doctoral program in marriage and family therapy. And I left Nietzsche behind in favor of American philosophy, especially Emerson and Thoreau. The damage, however, was already done. So, in one of our very few wise agreements, we decided to part ways: she married a bomber pilot who I can only hope does not read Kierkegaard, and I married Carol, a philosopher who loathed Nietzsche.

Carol is a Kantian, and Immanuel Kant is usually considered *the* German philosopher, but Nietzsche called him a "catastrophic spider"—a system maker who spun a web of idealism that had entangled too many good thinkers. Kant embodied the Enlightenment ideals of order, harmony, rationality, and, above all, duty—philosophical concepts Nietzsche spent his entire life trying to dismantle. Kant was interested in self-control, but it was a precise, passionless kind of control that Nietzsche claimed was perfectly fitted to Christian notions of piety and self-sacrifice. Kant was not one for hiking or extreme fasting. He took measured, repetitive walks, daily constitutionals that never ventured beyond the walls of his home of Königsberg. The townspeople were said to have set their watches by Kant's famous Philosopher's Walk. This sort of restricted perambulation was unthinkable to Nietzsche— the sure sign of a constipated mind. Describing Kant in his *Antichrist*, he writes:

> This nihilist [Kant] with his Christian dogmatic entrails considered pleasure an *objection*. What could destroy us more quickly than working, thinking, and feeling without any inner necessity, without any deeply personal choice, without pleasure—as an automaton of "duty"? This is the very recipe for decadence, even for idiocy. Kant became an idiot.

Carol could not have disagreed more. She was attracted to Kant's belief that freedom was keyed to our rational capacities rather than to the fickle passions that controlled the Romantics and the thinkers, like Nietzsche, who sought to extend their legacy. The emotions, according to Kant, more often than not led individuals astray by allowing them to confuse moral imperative with personal preference. When driven by their passions, individuals tended to overlook their moral duties and act irrationally. Carol thought Nietzsche was a marauding fool, or at least pathetically misguided.

By the time I met Carol, I'd almost gotten over Nietzsche. I'd nearly wrested myself from my obsession with hiking and fasting, embracing instead an American philosophy that attempted to balance self-determination with moral responsibility. The shift in philosophical focus was a decision, or an attempt, to change myself. American philosophers—Ralph Waldo Emerson, William James, Josiah Royce—continued the tradition of intellectual wandering and took to the mountains of New England in search of inspiration and concentration. But they often hiked together—with kindred intellectual spirits who could share in their philosophical projects. With their help, I slowly, haltingly learned to walk leisurely with someone else.

When one spends time reading—and falls in love with—a particular philosopher, he gradually begins to confuse the world of objective fact with an imagined one of ideals and beliefs. This is one of the true joys of reading philosophy—its danger but also its redemptive possibility. In leaving Nietzsche's mania behind and turning to the more measured sentiments of American thinkers, and even to Kant, I slowly found a way to live and, after some difficulty, to love. And I was much happier for it. I even wrote a book about the salvific effects of American philosophy, about how the love of wisdom could bring two people together. But on quiet nights, after a day of teaching Nietzsche, the high peaks once again began to beckon.

NIETZSCHE'S BREED OF FREETHINKER WAS, at least stereotypically, a very earnest cartoon of masculinity, a rule-breaker, a skeptic, in Emerson's words, "a nonconformist." I was supposed to be too old for this. Edging into my forties, there was a potential price to pay in following the philosophical iconoclast. Carol's invitation to return to Switzerland was, given the history of the place, admirably brave, but the idea of returning to the Alps with her summoned up a nightmarish premonition: a man in his intellectual prime who kills off his relationships—and nearly kills himself—in the midst of a manic spurt of productivity, on the edge of real or, more likely, imagined greatness. Nietzsche's Alps have the uncanny ability to heighten and deepen any buoyancy or downturn. I remembered his words from March 1883, after severing ties from family and friends and fleeing to Sils-Maria for the second time: "I've lost interest in everything . . . I feel so incomplete, so inexpressibly conscious of having bungled and botched my whole creative life." And three months later, on the brink of suicide: "I am now working like a man who is 'putting his house in order before departing.'"

As a teenager, I'd cherished these words from my companion in misery, but now, at the age of thirty-six, they just frightened me. If Carol and I followed Nietzsche into the mountains again and slipped or jumped, we now had something to lose: our daughter, Becca; students we loved; two rare jobs in philosophy; a quiet family farmhouse steps from Walden Pond; our health; a bit of respect from our colleagues; each other; and time to enjoy it all. At this point, traveling into the mountains might be nothing more than an act of ingratitude.

My thoughts, however, continued to gravitate to my long-neglected philosophical hermit. Nietzsche, the perennial bachelor, believed that marriage could take two distinct forms. It could, as he suggests, be just "one long stupidity," in which two desperate people mask their neediness with all the trappings of a conventional life. "Alas, this filth of the soul in pair!" Nietzsche cries. "Alas, this wretched contentment in pair!" When Carol and I married, we promised never again to perpetuate "this filth of the soul in pair." Her willingness to hike with me—to take the risk together—was a way to keep this promise. According to Nietzsche, marriage could be a prolonged mistake, but it could also embody something else, something higher: "[T]he will of two to create the one that is more than those who created it. Reverence for each other, as for those willing with such a will, is what I [Nietzsche] name marriage." This was, among other things, what we could look for in the mountains. Carol might have thought that Nietzsche was an idiot, but my onetime admiration for him mattered to her. She was more than curious: she wanted to understand.

I contacted the Nietzsche-Haus in Sils-Maria, and the curator assured me that they had a room—the one closest to Nietzsche's—the rough-paneled bedroom from my youth. I remembered its low ceiling and the unadorned walls that seemed to close in on a visitor as the evening hours passed. Carol and I could make do in tight quarters. I spent a month researching tickets and planning our route, but the scheme was still missing something—or rather someone. Nietzsche could travel across Europe, by himself or with an occasional friend, for weeks at a time. But Nietzsche was not a father.

It was decided: Becca would come too. She was, after all, the one who wanted to know what had happened to my ear. If Becca came, we would not be staying in the Nietzsche-Haus; it was one thing to terrorize Carol with its creepy rooms, but quite another to subject a four-year-old to life's macabre realities. We would keep the reservation at the museum-cum-hotel (I could sleep there when the spirit moved me) and camp throughout the month, but we needed to book alternative lodging. There was only one place I wanted to stay: the hotel on the hill behind the Nietzsche-Haus, where I dined on my last night in Sils-Maria.

When I was nineteen, I hadn't known, or noticed or cared, but the hotel had a name, a famous one: Das Waldhaus Sils.

This grande dame of a hotel—the "house in the woods"—had attracted a century's worth of Nietzschean pilgrims: Thomas Mann, Theodor Adorno, Carl Jung, Primo Levi, and, by far my favorite, Hermann Hesse. It is no exaggeration to say that it was the birthplace of post-Nietzschean philosophy, a space to experiment with a philosopher-hero's thoughts. Mann, Adorno, and Hesse had each spent months, and in some cases years, at the hotel. The jarring disjunction between the austerity of the Nietzsche-Haus and the luxury of Das Waldhaus was not lost on me, and I was of two minds about the decision to book the rooms. But somehow everything, even the deep ambivalence, felt right. It would give me a reason to reread Hesse's *Steppenwolf*, a story of a man's bifurcated nature, a book I'd always regarded as Nietzsche's most intimate biography.

THE LAST MAN

Man is a polluted river. One must be a sea to receive a
polluted river without becoming defiled.

—Friedrich Nietzsche,
Thus Spoke Zarathustra, 1883

O UR FAMILY WOULD FOLLOW NIETZSCHE INTO THE mountains, but first we had to face the airport and a transatlantic flight, which, I knew, would be the most tedious leg of the journey. Nietzsche became famous for his philosophy of the mountain, but he began his life as a thinker far from its height, by facing the deadening forces of modern civilization. His Zarathustra explains that the greatest obstacle to becoming *übermenschlich* is what he terms the "Last Man," a figure that represents the lifeless efficiency of the modern day. The Overman is the ideal of the future, of what human beings could eventually aspire to. But the Last Man stands in the way, and on that muggy evening in August, I was almost positive that he'd built, and now occupied, the lowlands of Logan International Airport.

Today, the lights from Logan's airstrips completely obscure the starry heavens, and the noise from the planes makes concentrating on anything nearly impossible. The airport's construction in the first half of the twentieth century involved bulldozing and paving the 2,384 acres of wetland that separate Boston from the Atlantic Ocean. At the time, a few free spirits living in the coastal plain protested, lying down in front of the dump trucks that were carting away the sand. Of course, the free spirits were carted away by police. Order was restored, and the beach was leveled in order to make way for six runways that serve thirty million travelers a year. All of them seemed to be at the airport when we arrived.

When transatlantic travel first began, the world was still large. Travelers who dared to traverse it were as likely to contract a disease and die as to arrive safely at a desired destination. But today "the earth has become small," writes Nietzsche, "and on it hops the Last Man." According to Zarathustra, the Last Man views safety and comfort as the root of all happiness. Life—like a red-eye flight—should pass as smoothly and painlessly as possible. " 'We have invented joy!' exclaims the last man. And he blinks." Nietzsche's time in Basel had taught him that there was something deadening and artificial about this contentment, and as I looked around Logan, it struck me that little had changed in the hundred and fifty years since his escape to Sils-Maria. In fact, it was difficult to remember that

Nietzsche had had high hopes for this country: the United States was the place, he thought, where individualism and freedom might actually take root. He wasn't entirely right about this.

We stepped onto the airport terminal's moving walkway, which carried us past an endless line of snack shacks, depositing us at the entrance to a mall where travelers could buy their essentials: inflatable neck pillows, electric blankets, phone chargers. The work of Nietzsche was nowhere in sight.

Clearly, sometime in the last century, America had followed Europe's lead in exchanging beauty and risk for comfort and convenience. Nietzsche, however, believed that this obsession with maintaining some semblance of health was far from actually being healthy. Agreeing with the Roman historian and philosopher Tacitus, Nietzsche wrote, "[I]n dealing with the human body, doctors have not much to say in praise of the patient who only keeps well by worrying about his health. Not being ill doesn't amount to much . . . If soundness is all you commend in him, he is really next door to an invalid." According to Nietzsche, there are two forms of health: the futile type that tries to keep death at bay as long as possible, and the affirming type that embraces life, even its deficiencies and excesses.

By the time he reached the age of thirty, Nietzsche was battling a host of physical ailments. While serving as a hospital attendant in the Franco-Prussian War, he had contracted diphtheria, dysentery, and what we now call post-traumatic stress disorder, and for much of the 1870s he searched in vain for cures. As his professorship at Basel came to a close, however, Nietzsche had begun to reconceive the meaning of health.

Returning to the ancient Greeks, he argued that their remarkable strength was born of *agon*—the friction of contest—which was far from comfortable. Being sick could be a condition to which one eventually succumbs, but it could also be a trial that is heroically endured. The Greeks, according to Nietzsche, didn't deny the existence of human suffering and limitation, but rather sought to transform them in art. In tragedy, characters lay hold of suffering and make it their own—claim it in such a way that failure and limitation become meaningful, indeed, gloriously so. Human existence is cruel, harsh, and painfully short, but the tragic heroes of ancient Greece found a way to make the suffering and sudden endings of life beautiful, or aesthetically significant. This is what Nietzsche meant in *The Birth of Tragedy* when he claimed that the existence can be justified only as an aesthetic experience.

Aesthetic experience—the experience of the beautiful and sublime—has often been regarded as beyond the purview of modern philosophers. As the scientific revolution gathered speed and tipped into the Age of Enlightenment, thinkers prioritized rational and moral ideals above all others. One's decisions and actions were to be guided by universal principles of prudence, logic, and reason rather than by any vague pursuit of the beautiful life. By contrast, Nietzsche believed that a quest for aesthetic experience was the only way to mitigate the horror of existence. The Greeks understood beauty in its most robust sense—as a way of transforming agony and drudgery into something creative and enrapturing. There was no such thing as "art for art's sake" for the Greeks; the point was to come to see the tensions and contradictions of life—even the despised and the hideous—as one would take in a work of art.

I glanced across the terminal to the flickering screens of a generic sports bar. The Tour de France was in full swing, and the riders, each of them powered by their own two legs, were in the Alps. Crashes, dehydration, torn tendons, broken bones: they were killing themselves on these mountains. And it was a thing of beauty. At Logan, a crowd of beer-drinking Americans had gathered to eat burgers and watch. There are still traces of the tragic struggle in our culture, but they are faint. High-stakes competition is regarded as mere spectacle rather than as a vital part of everyday life. We wedged ourselves into the restaurant, ordered Becca dinner, had a drink, and let the time until our departure pass as pleasantly as possible, entertained by two-dimensional images of riders traversing the peaks and valleys.

Somewhere in the course of the next hour I lost *Zarathustra*. I scoured the bar, the bathrooms, and the other shops, but it was no use. He was gone. My companion for so many years, a weathered friend for all seasons, had finally abandoned me. Carol assured me that I could find another copy of the book when I arrived. Our plane began to board, and we followed our companions, single file, to the gate, where we presented our boarding passes and then made our way to the gangway and our assigned seats. Becca slid in between us, and we prepared for the long haul. A large man shoved himself into a nearby row and got comfortable—pillows, blankets, fleecy socks, noise-canceling headphones, sleeping pills. The Last Man blinked twice, gave me a sleepy, meaningless smile, and was gone before the plane took off. I too leaned back, pulled Becca onto my lap, and did my best to relax, but I couldn't rid myself of what Nietzsche called *"unzeitgemässe Betrachtungen"*: inappropriate ideas, thoughts out of season.

UNZEITGEMÄSSE BETRACHTUNGEN, often translated as Nietzsche's *Untimely Meditations*, consumed his thirties. He would later reflect that these essays served to vent "everything negative and rebellious that is hidden within me." A double-edged theme pervades the *Meditations*: a vicious rejection of the intellectual, political, and cultural establishment of Western Europe and a pledge to defend an alternative "picture of life." He would paint this "picture" with the help of Schopenhauer's pessimism, which had, in Nietzsche's words, "an ideal in the background, a powerful masculine seriousness, an aversion to that which is hollow and without substance and an affection for health and simplicity." Pessimism disabused him of the idea that everyday life was meaningful and prepared him for the pursuit of higher goals—to entertain, at least for a moment, the possibility of transcendence. Nietzsche, for a time, believed that this transcendence would be embodied in the Romantic music of Richard Wagner.

Nietzsche had met Wagner as he prepared to embark on his professorial life at Basel. He was in search of a mentor and a way to escape the strictures of academic thinking; Wagner was in search of a protégé who could defend his music in print. At their first meeting, deep in philosophical conversation, a bond was forged, and Wagner invited the young man to his summer home at Tribschen, on the shores of Lake Lucerne. Nietzsche accepted, initiating a series of trips, a dozen in total after 1869, that defined his early commitment to Romanticism. Broadly speaking, the Romantics believed that the point of life was to find oneself in nature, to be inspired by the spirit of the cosmos, to explore the deepest subjective feelings—aesthetic, moral, and spiritual—in the face of nature's universality. Wagner's home at Tribschen was arranged to promote this form of self-discovery. The composer reserved a guest room for his aspiring acolyte. Remarking on his first days with Wagner, Nietzsche wrote, "I can only say that no cloud ever darkened the sky above our heads."

The academic world in Basel was blinkered and scientific, driven by a tedious hierarchy and the false pretenses of high culture. It was, in Nietzsche's words, a "dog kennel" where conformity and obedience were demanded and rewarded. The world that the Wagners created in Lucerne, in stark contrast, was extraordinary, mythological, imaginary—populated by muses and angels. Wagner's realm was pointedly antimodern, built on the belief that the only way to save the hideous present was to worship the beauty of the distant past. This squared with Nietzsche's instincts as a philologist, and he would, for a time, become Wagner's greatest champion. In *Human, All Too Human*, Nietzsche writes that "if you do not have a good father, you should procure one." A good father: this is what he tried—and ultimately failed—to find in Wagner.

Finding a place at Lucerne, however, wasn't easy. Nietzsche was still the son of a conservative mother, which made allying himself with the composer somewhat difficult. Wagner had just sired his third illegitimate child with Cosima von Bülow (daughter of Franz Lizst), and this impropriety initially made the young professor uneasy. When the couple finally married, Wagner joked that the wedding made no one happier than Nietzsche, who had remained "unnaturally reserved" around the illicit lovers. The Wagners' marriage in the summer of 1870 therefore signaled an uptick in the philosopher's dedication to their artistic agenda. Like so many reverential relationships, Nietzsche's affection for the composer was highly dysfunctional. Wagner drafted a hit list of his musical opponents and assigned Nietzsche the role of intellectual assassin, a position the young man dutifully filled in the early years of their relationship, becoming the philosophical spokesperson of the Bayreuth movement, the elaborate plan to transform a nondescript Bavarian village into a Romantic mecca. When the foundations for the grand opera house were laid in 1872, Nietzsche was there, proudly declaring himself a "Wagnerian philosopher." *The Birth of Tragedy*, published in the same year, was largely dismissed by the traditional philological community of Basel but embraced by Wagner's followers as a manual for reviving European culture. Cosima congratulated Nietzsche on the treatise's success by putting it in its place as "the greatest source of *Wagnerian* knowledge," but her words were pointedly Janus-faced—congratulatory but admonishing. A son should be careful not to surpass his father's stature.

Nietzsche's popularity, in Cosima's mind, depended on his remaining derivative, the mouthpiece of her husband's genius. Nietzsche's was a fame dependent on servitude. By the time he finished his fourth *Untimely Meditation*, "Wagner in Bayreuth," the young professor was beginning to understand his situation, and his view of Wagner slowly shifted. His adopted father was, the young man admitted, a "strange enigma," but one that—like a ghost or a god—still required reverence. Nietzsche's love, however, was only occasionally reciprocated, and when it was, Wagner's affections were never free.

"You are," Wagner wrote to Nietzsche in a moment of tenderness, "the only benefit that life has brought me." But in this case, in every case, the elderly man wanted something in return for his praise: this time the philosopher was to become the tutor of the Wagners' third child—their real child—Seigfried. "He needs you," Wagner wrote to Nietzsche, "the boy needs you." In many ways, Nietzsche was the needy one, and his "father" knew it. After the publication of *The Birth of Tragedy*, Wagner confided to his young protégé: "As I said to Cos., in my affections you come immediately after her." This might have been true, but such praise came with an equal share of abuse and degradation. As Nietzsche approached middle age, he became, quite literally, the Wagners' errand boy—sent to Basel's shops for caviar and apricot jam, to the bookbinder to rebind Richard's classic compositions, and to the clothier, in a testament to the intimacy of their relationship, to fetch the old man's underwear. In theory, the relationship between Nietzsche and the composer was to be one of empowerment and freedom, but in practice it often amounted to a not so subtle form of domination.

In the end, it is unsurprising that Wagner did little to alleviate the young Nietzsche's suffering or his general dis-ease with life. The composer was a miserable surrogate father—distant and withholding—but there was another, ostensibly philosophical problem. Nietzsche maintained that only aesthetic experience could justify existence and that the value of life was to be realized in a sensitivity and attunement to life's high notes but also to its faintest pitches. Before he escaped to the mountains of Sils-Maria, he came to believe that Wagner lacked this nuance and care, that very little of his supposed artistry was actually aesthetically pleasing. Silence and crescendo, silence and crescendo—Wagner takes his listener through repeated cycles of despair and redemption. It was flashy but, Nietzsche ultimately concluded, largely without substance. This brutal catharsis has its appeal, and the petite bourgeoisie adored it, but one can grow tired of the cycle, and Nietzsche did. At one point when Wagner was still unsure of his success, he reflected that the emotional effect of his operas might be achieved with no music at all, and he might have been right. The score is additive, not constitutive, in Wagner's grand theatrical productions. As Nietzsche began to turn on Wagner, he wrote:

> Wagner's art is sick. The problems he presents on the stage—all of them problems of hysterics—the convulsive nature of his affects, his overexcited sensibility, his taste that required ever stronger spices, his instability which he dressed up as principles, not least of all the choice of his heroes and heroines—consider them as physiological types (a pathological gallery!)—all of this taken together represents a profile of sickness that permits no further doubt . . .

Above all—and this was the definitive point for the philosopher—the performances, in all their grand stupidity, required blind devotion. Going to a Wagner opera in the late 1870s wasn't very different from attending a religious service or a pep rally, and the composer was all too happy to serve simultaneously as its high priest and master of ceremonies. In the wake of the German victory in the Franco-Prussian War, the Bayreuth Festival, initiated in 1876, emerged as a type of religio-political cult in which German patriotism was tied inextricably to a certain form of zealous Protestantism. According to Nietzsche, the composer had become a salesman or national hero rather than a genuine artist of life. This wasn't entirely of Wagner's doing, but he and his new wife loved the stardom they quickly achieved. The superiority of the Teutonic culture, according to many Germans, was preordained from on high, and Wagner's operas were taken to be the ultimate celebration of God and country.

All this left Nietzsche disgusted. What had started as a private conversation in Leipzig about philosophy and nonconformity had morphed into optimistic nationalism and religious dedication in the Bayreuth Wagner-fest a decade later. What had promised to be a self-affirming relationship had become a form of self-abnegation in the name of idol worship. What had started as a matter of creativity and inner expression had become a commodity of wide appeal but, ultimately, of questionable value. This was, for Nietzsche, a grand betrayal of friendship. Describing the first gathering at Bayreuth, he recounted, "We found Wagner again, draped in German 'virtues.'" The audience—a growing number of fanatics—made opera, the highest form of aesthetic expression, into a crass national pastime. "The Wagnerian," in Nietzsche's words, "had become the master over Wagner—*German* art, the *German* master, *German* beer."

Aesthetic experience could justify human existence but could also, just as easily, invalidate it. The mass production and consumption of art could be used to distract, mask, or blind an audience. By 1878, when Nietzsche fully broke with Wagner, he was well aware of this danger: the zealots at Bayreuth "require Wagner as an opiate: they forget themselves, they are rid of themselves for a moment . . ." This is what salvation amounted to for many Germans of the time: to lose themselves

in the blaring sound of a patriotic, Christian spectacle. Nietzsche was completely galled, and his writings from the late 1870s
onward were tinged with this disaffection. Nietzsche's entrap-
ment by and subsequent estrangement from Wagner was de-
cisive in his retreat into the mountains, the backstory to his
epic hiking.

SUNLIGHT BEGAN TO SHINE beneath the window shades of
the plane. We were almost there. Becca, fast asleep, shifted in
my arms. She was a beautiful, lovable child—who was being
held too tightly. Loosening my grip, I closed my eyes.

Wagner had drawn Nietzsche in slowly, almost indiscern-
ibly. I could understand that. Before loathing my father, I'd
wanted to *be* him: after all, he was dashing and charismatic,
and elusive, and therefore worthy of worship, especially by
a child.

When I was four, and for the next six years, Jan occasionally told me that he'd never wanted children but that I was not
always the burden he'd anticipated. I came to remember—and
indeed cherish—these strange moments that hovered somewhere between shame and pride.

Before we finally disowned each other, Jan would swoop
in for a weekend visit, to dress us up in country club outfits, to
pluck us out of our mundane life with our mother, to take us
to the Devon Horse Show to watch his girlfriend compete. This
was supposed to be a treat, an exceptional outing for exemplary
children. We'd sit quietly on a red plaid blanket and clap—but
not too much—as the riders took the domesticated animals

through their paces. Even then, I felt for the horses. The tweed was itchy and constrictive, but we wore it dutifully, even happily. Only very lucky children got to be this uncomfortable and embarrassed. Subjugation had its pleasures. It was in Wagner's company that Nietzsche learned a lesson that he would pass on to his readers—that our deep desires for beauty and affection often stem from deprivation, melancholy, and pain.

Confined to my seat in the plane, I tried to relax my arms, to let go, to catch a moment of sleep, to think only of mountains.

THE ETERNAL
RETURN

*The question in each and every thing, "Do you want this
again and innumerable times again?"*

—Friedrich Nietzsche,
The Gay Science, 1882

AFTER NIETZSCHE'S FAMILY DISINTEGRATED WHEN
he was a young boy, he turned to his education as the
place from which to tap meaning. When, in his youth, scholarly distinction had been achieved but proved disappointing,
he turned to high art. When, in his middle age, high art showed
itself as a meaningless farce, he turned to—or into—himself.

The year was 1877. He was about to reach the mountains
of Sils-Maria. He was thirty-three. Years later, Nietzsche

reflected on this period of limbo, between his early and later writings, as a crucial moment of self-discovery. He went to the mountains, not to deviate from Wagner or civilization on the whole but to find, or return, to his own path:

> What reached a decision in me at that time was not a break with Wagner . . . [instead] I was overcome by impatience with myself; I saw that it was high time for me to recall and reflect on myself. All at once it became clear to me in a terrifying way how much time I had already wasted . . . It was then that my instinct made its inexorable decision against any longer yielding, going along, and confounding myself.

This moment of self-discovery was also one of great sickness. Nietzsche's health had declined precipitously, and now migraines and nausea were his nearly constant companions. Strangely, he remarked that this sickness—still to this day unexplained—was the guide that led him back to himself. "Sickness," he explained, "detached me slowly [from society]: it spared me any break, any violent and offensive step . . . My sickness also gave me the right to abandon all my habits completely, it commanded me to *forget*." It gave Nietzsche the right to forget the strictures of Basel and the betrayals of Bayreuth, but it also allowed the young scholar to remember, or take account, of his own most personal history. It was a period of recovery, in the most literal sense, a time to gather himself up, to regain possession of what had been nearly lost in his time in school and with Wagner. He writes that regaining his physical health—what most of us term "recovery"—was but a consequence of this philosophical undertaking.

The books Nietzsche dashed off during this time were unlike the philosophical tomes he'd produced as a young man. *Human, All Too Human*, published in 1878, and *The Dawn of Day*, which emerged three years later, consisted of collections of aphorisms, short jottings that defy a reader's desire to make them cohere. They are but germs of future thoughts that Nietzsche would spend the rest of his life developing and unleashing. They are, I take it, his first attempt to give voice to the forbidden, the truths that modernity would rather not face. "No one dies of fatal truths these days," Nietzsche writes in *Human, All Too Human*, "there are too many antidotes." These books were meant to lower our defenses, to make us susceptible to the philosophy that he would write in the Alps, particularly his *Zarathustra*. Of *The Dawn*, Nietzsche writes, "With this book my campaign against morality begins."

On my first trip to the mountains, I'd embraced this battle cry with teenage exuberance. My childhood had been a relatively happy one under my mother's watchful eye, but her vigilance, heightened by my father's absence, grated on me and my brother as we became young men. We were expected to be so very "good." I didn't necessarily want to be "bad" (perhaps I was still too young or too afraid for that), but I thrilled at my new acquaintance with a thinker who drew into question the very notion of good and evil. To think that the "good" wasn't good at all! My excitement, however, was misplaced—or rather, premature. Understanding *The Dawn* was, for Nietzsche, a subtler and less bellicose challenge. This, I now understand, is what he meant when he said that the book did not "smell in the least of powder"—gunpowder, that is.

This was not a time for fighting, but rather of recovering. I'd missed this as a teenager: the way that Nietzsche was, in his own words, "preparing a moment of the highest self-examination for humanity, a great noon when it looks back and far forward, when it emerges from the dominion of accidents and priests and for the first time poses, as a whole, the question of Why? and For What?" I was still struggling, wresting, asserting, but had yet to take up the more challenging task—one that Nietzsche came to before arriving in Sils—of knowing and then revaluing myself.

The "revaluation of values" is touted as one of Nietzsche's greatest contributions to the history of philosophy. Instead of taking ethical norms—such as humility, pity, and self-sacrifice—at face value as guides to right action, Nietzsche asks the subversive question: Where did these values *come from* in the first place? What is their background? What is their forgotten history? The very intimation that morals came from somewhere, that they had an origin and were not given absolutely and for all time, is a radical philosophical move. It suggests that ethical life could be otherwise and that the fixity of social norms and mores is unshakably contingent. Revaluing life, according to Nietzsche, turns on one's ability to live in the face of this reality.

The revaluation of values gains traction in the initial, relatively simple insight that "humanity is *not* all by itself on the right way, that it is by no means governed divinely, that, on the contrary, it has been precisely among its holiest value concepts that the instinct of denial, corruption, and decadence has ruled seductively." The good is but a prejudice, often harmful, that needs to be stripped bare and reexamined. In other words, one is to dispense with the metaphysical fictions—the religion and ideology—that has governed much of human existence. This, unfortunately, is the easy part. The revaluation of values, however, turns on a second commitment or undertaking: when the ground of morality has been cleared and prejudice has been razed, a thinker is left to question the ultimate worth of human existence. Without traditional metaphysics and religion, one is delivered—or returned—to the natural world and is charged to make meaning in this rugged landscape. Finally, the most formidable step: to promote power and life, the two driving forces of nature, in such a way as to avoid the stultifying ways of the past. Hard, harder, hardest—and it took Nietzsche a decade in the mountains to think it through.

We would have thirteen days in Sils-Maria. It wasn't much, I knew, but something could be accomplished. Nietzsche had finished the first three parts of *Thus Spoke Zarathustra* in the same amount of time.

WE DEPLANED IN ZÜRICH, the spiritual doppelgänger of Nietzsche's Basel, which is to say wholly spiritless, and we left as quickly as possible. This time, by car. The road to Sils-Maria is a long one, and after a sleepless night it felt even longer—a hundred and twenty-five miles, which, with a toddler in tow, took just over four hours. I could have traveled faster by myself. But as we approached Chur and I realized the path I was retracing, this thought quickly vanished. The last time I was here, I remembered, I tried to travel by myself and nearly died. The journey, between Chur, Splügen, and the

Nietzsche-Haus—between slicing my heel open, getting lost, and developing frostbite—had taken me many days.

Chur hadn't changed. Indeed, in many respects it never has. It's been continuously occupied since the Bronze Age, five thousand years ago, and the signs of this enduring inhabitancy are everywhere. "We need history," Nietzsche tells his reader, "inasmuch as the past wells up in us in hundreds of ways. Indeed we ourselves are nothing other than what we sense at each instant of that onward flow." In 1464 Chur burned to the ground, but when German artisans rebuilt it in subsequent years, new buildings were laid on the foundations of the old. The city, unlike so many modern ones, does not assault the landscape but settles gently in the valley between vaulting mountains. This too was a matter of being situated in, or on, the past—a deep foundation of glacial stone.

We arrived on a cool Sunday in mid-August, and I remembered Nietzsche's letter to his mother upon his arrival: "Sabbath peace and an afternoon mood prevailed in the town of Chur. I walked up the main road at a leisurely pace; as on the previous day, everything lay before me transfigured . . ." *Transfigured*. That is a better word than *changed*, which connotes becoming something wholly different. This was more akin to shape-shifting, but the shift preserved something of the past. Becca looked up and out the window of the car, to a road high above us. We'd be there soon. And I was, this time, so glad to see the guardrails.

When I was nineteen, I left Chur behind and took the Via Mala—literally, the "bad road"—to Splügen. This was, after all, the exact route Nietzsche had taken in 1872, and I had wanted to follow it exactly. But now the three of us didn't have the time—or the energy—for the bad road, and we would cut directly on Route 3 to the Julier Pass and then descend to Silva-plana and Sils-Maria. Sometimes deviations from the past are necessary or preferable.

There was roadwork, so it was stop-and-start, which I found rather annoying until I realized that these interruptions were the only way a driver could actually appreciate the views. A single hiker, a young man in a black poncho and sneakers carrying a light pack, passed us as we waited for a workman to wave us through. His gait was easy, but his ex-posed calves were striated in a way that told me he'd been on the road for many days. Was he hitchhiking? For a minute I considered lowering the window, calling him back, asking if he needed a ride to the top. A strange impulse, I knew, that had absolutely nothing to do with his well-being and not a little to do with my own. The tramper cut sharply uphill, off the road, and was gone.

As we approached the Julier Pass, at 7,494 feet, I was drawn once again to the mountains that loomed above us. They seemed so very close. At the next construction stop I thought I caught sight of my hiker cresting a rise in the dis-tance. This stop was longer than the others—a group of men were digging up the black macadam with the help of a steam shovel. Eight inches beneath our road were stones, perfectly cubed and set out in rows, that had been laid in 1840. They were surprisingly close to the surface. When we reached the "top," which was really just the bottom of another mountain valley, we passed two stone pillars jutting out of the earth, column stumps from an ancient Roman temple. Today, trav-elers touch the stones with their right hands for good luck as they continue their journey, descending into the Engadine below.

"OF ALL THE PLACES on Earth, I feel best here in the Engadine," Nietzsche wrote. "To be sure, the attacks come to me here as they do everywhere else; yet they are milder by far, much more humane. I am continuously calmed here, none of the pressure that I feel everywhere else." Many writers who have followed in Nietzsche's footsteps have come to understand the meaning of these words. The Engadine, with its woods, lakes, and meadows, are, in Nietzsche's words, "as though made for me." Here, one can find, on precious occasion, a deep fittedness between the past and the present, between human selfhood and the vast, often terrifying expanse of nature.

The Alpine valley of the Upper Engadine stretches eight miles from the Maloja Pass, on the edge of the Italian border, northeast, across three crystal-blue lakes—Sils, Silvaplana, and St. Moritz—and terminates in the hotel-studded city of St. Moritz, a well-known destination of the rich and famous. The road construction ended, and we picked up the pace as we rolled toward Silvaplana. After the switchbacks of the Julier Pass, the stretch between Silvaplana and Sils-Maria was a welcome relief. It curves gently around the lake, which, on most days, is ruffled by the wind. But on that day it was completely still, creating a perfect emerald table on which the mountains were firmly set. When the glaciers flowed through these valleys in ice ages, they excavated the land, and over time, the water filled in the massive depressions that were created. How many years, how many rains, day after day, did it take to fill such a lake?

The car was quiet. Becca had fallen asleep on the descent, and Carol and I were alone with the lake, the mountains, and a blessed moment of calm. I'd fallen in love with her in the White Mountains of New Hampshire, a hidden place where we'd escaped two marriages that really deserved to die. I caught sight of the wooded hills above Sils-Maria and, above the trees, the white turret of the Waldhaus. There was no running away now—just an uncanny sort of homecoming.

"Jesus Christ." Carol breathed deeply and let it out at once. "That's sublime."

These were not the White Mountains. I couldn't see it from the car, but I knew what traced the edge of the road we were traveling: the walking path that I frequented in my youth, the same one that carried Nietzsche to his *Zarathustra*. When he walked this trail, skirting the water, Nietzsche wrote that he frequently wept "not sentimental tears, but tears of exultation." When you read Nietzsche in a library or a coffee shop, it is possible to misinterpret this as hyperbole or the ravings of a madman. But not here. There is no such thing as hyperbole in the Alps. "The intensities of my feeling," he claimed, "make me shudder and laugh aloud."

On the opposite shore of the lake, on a small outcropping of grass, sits a single pyramidal stone. I remembered it as shoulder height, although I now know it is considerably larger, almost twice the size of a man, mirroring, in miniature, the surrounding mountains. When I first saw it, I tried unsuccessfully to climb it. This rock is perhaps the best reason to read Nietzsche. It is, I am sure, the one and only reason I agreed to return to Switzerland. "Now I shall relate the history of Zarathustra," Nietzsche prepares his reader in *Ecce Homo*. Continuing, he explains:

The fundamental conception of this work, the idea of *eternal recurrence*, this highest formula of affirmation that is at all attainable, belongs in August 1881: it was penned on a sheet with the notation underneath "6000 feet beyond man and time." That day I was walking through the woods along the lake of Silvaplana; at a powerful pyramidal rock not far from Surlei I stopped. It was then that this idea came to me.

We didn't stop at the rock but continued into the hamlet of Sils-Maria, past the post office and the single grocery store, to the Hotel Edelweiss. Behind the hotel, tucked against the wooded hill just as I remembered it, was the Nietzsche-Haus. The door and shutters had been repainted the same color. Nothing, after seventeen years, appeared to have changed. It was not the pyramidal rock where Nietzsche conceived of the eternal recurrence, but it would do. The idea is a wonderful, awful one:

> *What if* some day or night a demon were to steal into your loneliest loneliness and say to you: "This life as you now live and have lived it you will have to live once again and innumerable times again; and there will be nothing new in it, but every pain and every joy and every thought and sigh and everything unspeakably small or great in your life must return to you, all in the same succession and sequence— even this spider and this moonlight between the trees, and even this moment and I myself . . ."

Indeed, "what if?" Nietzsche's demon is giving voice to an age-old metaphysical suggestion, namely that the movement of reality is best described in terms of cycles and epicycles, a snake devouring itself. Hinduism and Buddhism, each in its own varied way, express something similar in the doctrine of karma. Everything happens by way of repetition. A building crumbles and is rebuilt on the same site. Glaciers move day after day, so do rains, and lives. The old gives birth to the new, which immediately, at varying rates, becomes old.

Schopenhauer, Nietzsche's hero, expresses something of this cosmic point but explains that to take it seriously is often to face its debilitating psychological effects. In his *Studies in Pessimism*, he writes, "He who lives to see two or three generations is like a man who sits some time in the conjurer's booth at a fair, and witnesses the performance twice or thrice in succession. The tricks were meant to be seen only once; and when they are no longer a novelty and cease to deceive, their effect is gone." Nietzsche largely agreed and thought that most of us, most of the time, would be crushed by such an idea—to repeat this, and everything, ad infinitum. To relive the regret, the tedium, the disappointment of a single life over the course of an indefinite future, this would be truly hellish.

Past the Nietzsche-Haus, across the river that bisects Sils, up three steep switchbacks, three identical sections of road that took us above the town: finally we arrived, once again, at the Waldhaus. Nietzsche's demon wasn't finished on the topic of eternal return. It is more than just a metaphysical description or, in Schopenhauer's case, an explanation of why life is so dreadfully monotonous. It is a challenge—or, better, a question—that is to be answered not in words but in the course of life: "The question in each and every thing, 'Do you want this again and innumerable times again?' would lie on your actions as the heaviest weight! Or how well disposed would you have to become to yourself and to life *to long for nothing more fervently* than for this ultimate eternal confirmation and seal?"

Are we, in the words of William Butler Yeats, "content to live it all again"? Being content in this sense is not being distracted from, or lulled to sleep by, or resigning oneself to a fate that cannot be avoided. It is to live to your heart's *content* with the knowledge that you will do this, and everything, again, forever. We made our last turn into the Waldhaus driveway and came to rest beneath its canopied entryway. Nietzsche suggests that the affirmation of the eternal return is possible only if one is willing and able to become well-adjusted to life and to oneself.

To be well-adjusted, for Nietzsche, is to choose, whole-heartedly, what we think and where we find and create meaning. The specter of infinite monotony was for Nietzsche the abiding impetus to assume absolute responsibility: if one's choices are to be replayed endlessly, they'd better be the "right" ones. It might be tempting to think that the "rightness" of a decision could be affixed by some external moral or religious standard, but Nietzsche wants his readers to resist this temptation. Nietzsche's demon, after all, comes to us when we are all alone, his question can be heard only in one's "loneliest loneliness," and therefore the answer cannot be given by consensus or on behalf of some impersonal institutions. It is, indeed, the most personal of answers—the one that always determines an individual choice. Of course you can choose anything you want, to raise children or get married, but don't pretend to do it because these things have some sort of intrinsic value—they don't. Do it solely because you chose them and are willing to own up to them. In the story of our lives, these choices are ours and ours alone, and this is what gives things, all things, value. Only when one realizes this is he or she prepared to face the eternal recurrence, the entire cycle, without the risk of being crushed. Only then is one able to say with Yeats, "[A]nd yet again," and truly mean it.

For a long time, I thought that the "eternal return" was best understood as the *ouroboros*, the ancient symbol of infinity, a snake eating its own tail. Vicious and all-consuming, eternity destroys and creates in equal measure. The animal tries in vain to get ahold of itself but, in so doing, pulls only farther away. But perhaps the "eternal return" didn't always have to be this bleak and sinister. When you walk toward the mountains through Alpine valleys, you sometimes pass ancient farmhouses. They're nothing particularly special. After a while they all look the same. But they're not. On the sides of some of them, above doorframes and under windows, worn down by countless seasons, is a carving—primeval and reassuring. Three rabbits, conjoined by interlocking ears, chasing one another in a perpetual merry-go-round. These "three hares" are everywhere: from twelfth-century Mongol metalwork in Iran, to medieval churches in Devon, England, to eighteenth-century synagogues in Germany. *Shafan, shafan, shafan*, in Hebrew. The symbol is radially symmetrical, fluid, and ongoing. The hares are a sign of rebirth. They are also a puzzle expressed in the ancient German riddle: "Three hares sharing three ears, but every one of them has two." Look carefully—it is, indeed, an optical illusion. Some people call it an impossible object, like the Penrose tribar or Escher's etchings. As we pulled up in front of the Waldhaus, I thought about the symbol: puzzling but not necessarily disturbing—a bit like déjà vu.

I PUT THE CAR IN PARK in the hotel driveway, slid the keys into my trouser pocket, and only then realized that I had not changed out of the pants I'd worn on the airplane. Becca had enjoyed part of her dinner and then dumped the rest down my front during a patch of turbulence. At least the milk had dried. I looked terrible and smelled worse. You must do one last thing in order to master the eternal recurrence. Just one: embrace even the most undesirable parts of existence—atrocities both momentous and minuscule. Many of life's occurrences are not choices at all. They happen suddenly and without warning—a great deluge, an accident that covers or drowns us, but in Nietzsche's words, "before fate strikes us, we should guide it."

"Is this it?" inquired a small voice from the back seat.

Yes, it was.

On my first visit to the Waldhaus, I was too malnourished and then too drunk to take note of the details. It was built in 1908, in the same year that Nietzsche's *Twilight of the Idols* was reprinted in a gilt, art nouveau binding that most scholars assume he would've abhorred. He probably would have passed similar judgment on the Waldhaus. During his stay in Sils-Maria, Nietzsche was drawn to a simplicity that often pitched into austerity.

"He wouldn't have stayed here!" joked Urs Kienberger, a gracious, quiet man in his sixties and one of the family members who owned the hotel. Kienberger would be our guide through the Waldhaus's lengthy history, one that we discovered was not unlike that of Chur or other places that have been passed down from one generation to the next. On the night we arrived, Kienberger greeted us by name in the foyer. He would never have used the word *owner*; he described himself instead as the "innkeeper." At first I thought this was false modesty or grand understatement, but as he explained, it made more sense. Beneath the imposing fairy-tale castle facade, the Waldhaus has only a hundred and forty rooms, which are paired with a hundred and forty–some staff. The hotel is not for passing through; it is an "inn," like "come *in* and stay awhile." Many intellectuals, such as Adorno, Mann, and Hesse, did.

Becca pattered through the oak-paneled foyer, across the marble floor and a bright red Oriental carpet, the vibrancy of which seemed out of sync with its apparent age. The hotel has been in Kienberger's family for six generations—perhaps, over time, they learned how to keep the carpet, which led through every hall of the massive building, magically clean. He was, it turned out, a "keeper" after all, a steward of a place that was meant to be untimely: it was something from the past that promises to remain, largely untouched, in the future. "It's not a museum," he protested, anticipating my thought. "It's alive, but it lives by not changing too much. A rock in the middle of a river perhaps."

Built before, and spared by, the devastation of World War I, the Waldhaus came of age in the Roaring Twenties. But it wasn't, like so many hotels of this era, built *for* this era. "It is a grand hotel," Kienberger said in passing, "but it's not opulent." Opulence distracts, its shiny bells and whistles are meant to take us beyond the mundane affairs of life, to deliver us elsewhere. The Waldhaus was not blinding or distracting.

It offered, according to our innkeeper, a "luxury of space": the space to explore, the space to reflect, the space to leave, the space to settle in—just space. In our world, the one packed with things and possessions, this space is often filled. Indeed, it is only valued when it is filled up—that is to say, when it is destroyed. Space *qua* space is completely impractical and a rare luxury indeed. I'm not sure how Kienberger read my mind—perhaps that is what a man in his profession learns to do—but as the tour ended and our stay began, he took us aside for a final word. Obviously the life of a hotel depends on certain practicalities—the tea has to arrive on time so that it remains hot. But—he gestured down the long hallway that terminated in a window that opened out into the valley—"it would be a great pity if everything was practical."

The tour of the Waldhaus terminated at the room where we, or at least Becca and Carol, would be staying. I'd still not decided where I would spend my first night in Sils-Maria. We'd somehow been upgraded, free of charge, to Room 244, overlooking the lake. It had a lock, but it wouldn't have to be used. The room was called, and surely was, the Bellavista, the "good view." The contrast between this view and the Via Mala was stark. When I was nineteen, on my way here, outside of Splügen I'd peered over the edge of a narrow bridge that spans a famous gorge between Andeer and Thusis. The bridge was only ten feet wide, but it was hundreds of feet to the bottom of the ravine. I looked over the edge and, for the first time, realized that vertigo is the dizziness associated not with fear of falling but with fear of willfully jumping. In the sheer openness, one can choose so many things. This was the knowledge, the feeling that grew so rapidly on my first trip to Sils-Maria.

The Bellavista was enclosed and protected, and at least at the moment, I relished the difference. The famous clouds of Sils-Maria roll down the Maloja Pass, snake around the mountains, and make their way with astonishing rapidity down the valley. Our window was nearly at the tree line, and the clouds and sun poured in. "I do not look out," writes Albert Ziegler, a Jesuit and longtime guest of the hotel, "the lake landscape of the Upper Engadine looks into the room. If I step back, the square of the window forms the frame of a picture whose colors and forms I am capable of looking at but not describing." Even Becca was dumbstruck. The three of us sat at the wide desk at the window, eating our dinners, and let the light pass into our room until darkness slowly crept in.

Remo Fasani, the poet and Dante scholar, adored this hotel and village, but he suggested that one need not love it for exactly the same reason that Nietzsche loved Sils-Maria:

Nietzsche, over a hundred years ago,
Came here in search of solitude and silence.
Here he received the gift of Zarathustra,
The superman who breaks down time itself.

Over the summers, I too have come here;
Here I spend time with silence and myself.
I write verses and I try in writing
To join the new with what has been of old.

Nietzsche wanted the ultimate in change:
To set the past ablaze, a funeral pyre
With which to usher in a brave new world

What I want, instead, is that the past live
In the present and in the future both
And that all time again vibrate as one.

Fasani, I am afraid, is wrong about this. Nietzsche wanted this as well: to have the past live in the present and in the future both, to have time again vibrate as one. This is the task of the eternal return. But it is—again, I am afraid—very hard. And when Nietzsche couldn't or didn't manage it, he was often happy or sad enough to set things ablaze.

PART II

ZARATHUSTRA
IN LOVE

What child would not have cause to weep over its parents?
Worthy I deemed this man and ripe for the sense of
the earth: but when I saw his wife, the earth seemed to me a
house for the senseless . . . This one went out like a hero
in quest of truths, and eventually he conquered a little
dressed up lie. His marriage he calls it.

—Friedrich Nietzsche,
Thus Spoke Zarathustra, 1883

I WOKE UP NEXT TO CAROL. AFTER THE DRIVE FROM Zürich and feeding and bathing Becca, I didn't have the energy or heart to be a real philosopher. I was steps from the Nietzsche-Haus, but it had seemed impossibly remote. I would get there in the coming days, I'd promised myself before curling up around Carol and letting myself and the day drift away.

But now I was wide-awake. It was 3:16 a.m. In my youth,

my mother called me "the prowler," a small nocturnal creature that would creep through the halls of our house at all hours of the night. She was, and still is, a model parent and would patiently, day after day, talk her prowler back to bed. "You should really sleep, Bear. You'll need your rest tomorrow," she'd say. I tried to listen. But I was always distracted by two voices, an internal dialogue between I and me that had begun when I was four or so, a few months after my father had left us.

Nietzsche's voices, and hence his insomnia, were relentless. "I and me are always too deeply in conversation," he admitted, "how could I endure it if there were not a friend?" The friend of the hermit, Nietzsche tells his reader, is always the third one, a bobber that keeps I and me from "sinking into the depths." For many years my mother had been that friend and life preserver, but as I edged toward adulthood, my prowling became more surreptitious—furtive.

Nietzsche is right: without a friend, it is possible to sink too deep. It is easier to stay on the surface with acquaintances, even loved ones; it allows one to breathe and deal with the practicalities of life. But sometimes one craves a bit of depth. I remembered Nietzsche's comment to his mother upon arriving in Sils-Maria, a direction not to tell his friends about his location. He didn't want visitors. Nietzsche's onetime bedroom was, according to Stefan Zweig, spare, filled with a single possession, "a heavy and graceless wooden trunk, packed with two shirts and a suit." Nothing else. "Otherwise only books and manuscripts and on a tray innumerous bottles and jars and potions . . . above all the dreadful sedatives to use against his insomnia, chloral hydrate and Veronal. A frightful arsenal of poisons and drugs but the only helpers in the empty silence of this strange room . . ." Despite the array of drugs, during the days when he wrote the first part of *Zarathustra*, Nietzsche hardly slept.

Three thirty-eight. Over the years, I've slowly learned how to use, or at least appreciate, insomnia. For a parent, it provides a blessed calm in an otherwise scattered existence. This was, in fact, the first solitary moment I'd had in days. Fatherhood is, by definition, a matter of togetherness. Even when you step back from the kids—which one hopefully does due to exhaustion or good judgment—they are with you always. Thankfully, they're usually so charming and buoyant that you don't mind that your individual, adult life has been hijacked or obliterated. But in the perfect silence of early morning it was almost possible to remember the solitude that was lost in becoming a parent. I pulled the blanket back, tucked it around Carol, slipped my legs out, and gingerly shifted my weight from the mattress to the floor. She didn't stir. Becca remained motionless. It was time for a walk.

The central hallway of the Waldhaus, with its off-white walls and blazing red carpet, stretches the length of the hotel, six hundred feet give or take. The building has three floors, so it would be a proper "explore." *An explore* is another one of my mother's terms. When my brother and I couldn't find anything productive to do during the summer doldrums, she would trundle us into the car and take us somewhere new to walk. Walk, not run—my mother is not one for running. These were slow meanders, with nowhere in particular to go. At first the pace infuriated me, but she explained—and then showed—that it really was the best way to see things. Things: trees, leaves, bugs, streams, ideas. Things that we, in our everyday lives, run past or intentionally step over. I slipped out of the Bellavista and went in search of Nietzsche.

WHEN NIETZSCHE CONCEIVED OF the eternal recurrence in the summer of 1881, he also began to think through a figure who might be able to shoulder its infinite responsibility, who would be able to own up to the decisions of life once and for all time. This wasn't Nietzsche himself—far from it—or even Zarathustra. It was the *Übermensch*, or Overman. Humanity, according to Zarathustra, is but a bridge or a rope that connects beasts to this superhuman ideal. It is something to be carefully, steadily traversed. In 1882, as Nietzsche began to direct his attention to this grand philosophical goal, he encountered a number of practical impediments that had to be addressed first. One of these obstacles was the difficulty of enduring love.

As the *Übermensch* took hold, so too did Nietzsche's ambivalence regarding companionship. All of this looks, from the outside, like a theoretical development in a man's outlook on life. But it's not. It was a theoretical breakthrough precipitated by the most jarring of personal breakups. Perhaps this interpretation verges on what is known as "the biographical fallacy"—the mistake of attributing the form and content of a piece of writing to the contours of the author's life. But in the case of Nietzsche, avoiding this fallacy seems impossible and unwise. "[B]ehind almost every word [of my *Zarathustra*]," Nietzsche writes, "there stands a personal experience, an act of self-overcoming of the highest order."

It all started in 1873, many years before Zarathustra made an appearance. Nietzsche was still very much with the Wagners, and his hopes for Romantic salvation were still at least partially alive. Then he met Paul Rée. He wrote to his friend Erwin Rohde of "a very reflective and talented man, a follower of Schopenhauer, by the name of Rée." The third child of a wealthy Jewish family, Rée studied philosophy in Leipzig and shared Nietzsche's interest not only in Schopenhauer but also in the history and the origins of morals. Having written his dissertation on Aristotle's *Ethics*, Rée was particularly fascinated by the virtue of altruism; he hypothesized that this caring for others was an inborn trait that had been selected by Darwinian evolution. Although Nietzsche came to reject this position, indeed quite adamantly in his *Genealogy of Morals*, he initially appreciated the alternative view, and the two young men became very close. Too close, at least for the comfort of the Wagners.

"The Jew," throughout the nineteenth century, was quickly becoming the scapegoat for a host of cultural and political ills. Wagner's anti-Semitism ran deep. He published *"Das Judenthum in der Musik"* ("The Music and the Jews"), first anonymously in 1850 and then again, under his own name, in 1869. It argued that Hebrew was a "creaking, squeaking, buzzing snuffle" that destroyed proper aesthetic feeling. This essay is now regarded as a landmark case of anti-Semitic literature, but it was just one among dozens of short essays that, until his death, Wagner wrote along these lines: German culture could be redeemed only in the total abandonment of Judaism. Rée was, for Wagner, an unwelcome addition to Nietzsche's small circle of friends.

When Nietzsche left Wagner's Bayreuth in 1876, it was literally with Rée in hand. Before the festival ended, the two escaped back to Basel, and Rée, five years Nietzsche's junior, took on the role of assistant and confidant. "We are very happy together," Nietzsche announced to his mother at the time. I have very little doubt that the men were, in fact, in love, as, I expect, are most best friends. Nietzsche's eyes plagued him during this time, so Rée would join him for hours in his darkened quarters, curtains drawn, shutters closed. And the rumors began to swirl in Bayreuth. What were these two single men doing in darkened chambers? Wagner had a theory, and he quietly spread it through the cultural circles of the Continent. Nietzsche's bad eyes were caused by excessive masturbation; his masturbation was caused by a pathological fear of having sex with women; his fear of women was caused by a hidden homosexuality; and his homosexuality explained Nietzsche's dark friendship with the Jew, Paul Rée. It was an absurd, malicious rumor, but one that continued to circulate for many years and was, at least in part, responsible for Nietzsche's escape to the mountains.

Perhaps Nietzsche could have escaped the rumor had he not insisted on prodding the musical monster one last time. "Here we are in Sorrento!" Nietzsche announced to his mother and sister in October 1876. Rée had joined him on the holiday, and the water was marvelous. There was only one problem: this was where the Wagners also vacationed. Nietzsche met Wagner for the last time in Sorrento on November 4. There is much dispute about the content of the conversation, but one thing is agreed: it was not wholly pleasant. Wagner's *Parsifal*, with all its explicitly masculine, Christian overtones, was undoubtedly mentioned if not discussed in detail, the perfect backdrop for parting ways with Nietzsche and his Jewish companion.

To love in spite of appearances can be one of the signs of true affection. In the midst of two divorces, this is how Carol and I began, in a rare moment when Nietzsche's *Beyond Good and Evil* had made perfect sense, even to my Kantian. To throw caution to the wind, to love with utter abandon (which amounts to the same thing), to endure the rumors of fair-weather friends, to almost intentionally form a relationship that is forbidden—this, Nietzsche learned from Rée, is to have succeeded. Rée would introduce Nietzsche to Lou Salomé in 1882, and this lesson would only deepen as they formed what Nietzsche called, with an irony that was lost on no one, "the trinity."

NIETZSCHE HAD PITIFULLY LITTLE LUCK when it came to love, but his failures in traditional courtship, by some accounts, were not failures at all but rather a function of his particularly high standards. He was, on occasion, very insightful about monogamous unions: "The best friend is most likely to be the best wife, since a good marriage is based on a talent for friendship." On other occasions, however, he seemed to echo Schopenhauer's unflinching sexism. "A woman may very well form a friendship with a man," Nietzsche concedes, "but for this to endure, it must be assisted by a little . . . antipathy." *Little* was not the word that many scholars use to describe his later antipathy toward women: "Woman has so much cause for shame; in woman there is so much pedantry, superficiality, schoolmasterliness, petty presumption, unbridledness, and indiscretion concealed . . . Alas, if ever the 'eternally tedious in woman'—she has plenty of it!—is allowed to venture forth!" In the same barbed passage he suggests that woman is best understood as a "possession," something that "must be cooped up to prevent it from flying away." Ultimately, the wife Nietzsche thought worthy of possession would be impossible to encage.

Nietzsche had first heard of Lou Salomé from Rée on March 13, 1882. Rée had met Salomé in Rome at the home of Malwida von Meysenbug, a mutual friend who organized a salon of young thinkers from around the Mediterranean. At the time, Meysenbug would also write to Nietzsche of Salomé, who "appears to me to have arrived at the same results in philosophical thinking as you, that is, towards a practical idealism, leaving behind every metaphysical presupposition and every concern about the explanation of metaphysical problems. Rée and I agree in the wish to see you with this extraordinary person . . ." Nietzsche was in love before even meeting the young Russian.

Nietzsche's beloved was a force of nature: mysterious, destructive, irresistible. "I found no more gifted or reflective spirit," he remarks after meeting Salomé in April 1882. "Lou is the smartest person I've ever met." He wasn't alone in his admiration. Rilke, who carried on a lifelong affair with her, attested to her greatness: "All that I am stirs me," he wrote to her, "because of you." Freud called her "the great understander" and repeatedly turned to her for intellectual guidance. Paul Rée, who introduced her to Nietzsche, was also in love with her and proposed to her at least once. She turned him down at least once. There was no need to marry, at least not yet. Lou was born in 1861, the daughter of a distinguished general in Czarist Russia; she had the means and freedom to travel and study through her early twenties; her admirers were numerous; and she relished the variety of experiences they afforded.

She was a brilliant philosopher in her own right and one of the first women to practice psychoanalysis.

It was an atypical relationship from the start. Nietzsche had serious philosophical work to do and misgivings about marriage, or at least a lengthy one, on the grounds that such a commitment would stifle his creativity. His smothering relationship with his mother and family had made him wary of new constraints. A two-year marriage, he told Rée prior to his meeting with Lou, was all he could muster, and then, he said, only "in view of what I have before me to accomplish in the next ten years." Still, Nietzsche recognized his desire for likeminded companionship. "I long for this type of woman . . . ," he admitted to Rée. By the end of March, the middle-aged Nietzsche had packed his bags and was on his way to Italy to complete an infamous love triangle.

Nietzsche might have discovered the idea of eternal recurrence on the pyramidal stone outside of Sils-Maria, but the inspiration for the twists of Zarathustra could have just as easily come to him at another sort of "rock" in Rome—at St. Peter's Basilica on the afternoon of April 26, 1882. He met Salomé, for the first time, in an empty confessional booth. "From what stars have we fallen to meet here?" According to Salomé, these were the first words Nietzsche uttered. The meeting was solemn, and Salomé writes that the philosopher's formal manners "fooled and flabbergasted" her. But things would become more informal, indeed wildly so, between the couple very soon. Nietzsche proposed to Salomé on their second meeting. "Too quickly," he explains, "does the lonely one extend his hand to those he encounters." She rejected him. He tried again, twice, with equal success.

In the spring of 1882, at the age of twenty-one, Salomé

proposed that Nietzsche and Rée join her as travel companions from Rome to her native Russia. Of course they accepted. They didn't make it all the way, but when they ultimately arrived in Lucerne, Nietzsche hired Jules Bonnet to take a staged photograph that captured something of their relationship: Salomé standing in a horse cart with a whip; Nietzsche and Rée, in the place of domesticated beasts, driven before her. Nietzsche was in love with a woman, perhaps for the first and only time. The trip was a return to Nietzsche's intellectual roots—back to Switzerland and Northern Italy—but this time with a woman he adored. The places were the same, but he hoped that the experience with Salomé would be different— that he could finally overcome the awkward isolation that had characterized most of his life and writing. The trip was different, but not in the way that the young man had hoped.

Nietzsche wanted nothing more than to find himself in Salomé, and it almost happened. In May, the couple hiked Monte Sacro, above Orta in the Italian Alps. Looking back on the hike, Salomé commented that this was, literally, the high point of their relationship. It was decidedly downhill from there. As their relationship intensified, so too did Nietzsche's philosophical speculations, which seemed to veer wildly from selfless abnegation to selfish megalomania, extremes that some men visit with regularity in early adulthood. Salomé couldn't remember whether the couple had kissed on the top of Monte Sacro, but she did recall what Nietzsche said, what he became, on the hike. In hushed tones, "with all the signs of the greatest horror," he recounted the story of eternal return. And then, according to his beloved, emerged the first sight of the Overman:

At first, he fashioned the mystical superior-human
ideal through self-intoxicated fantasy, dreams, and
rapture-like visions; and then, in order to save
himself from himself, he sought to identify himself
with them through one tremendous leap. Finally
he became a dual figure—half-sick and suffering;
half-saved; a laughing and superior human. The
one is like a creature, the other a creator; the one
assumes a reality and the other a mystical sur-reality.

This had always struck me as unnecessarily harsh. Nietzsche
is not alone in his twofold nature. For most human beings,
the gap between the real and the possible occasionally opens
to reveal precisely this bifurcation. But it was, I can only assume, a chasm for Nietzsche. He continued to want, and now
imagine, more than he could ever have.

To an onlooker, this sort of psychic fracturing is rather unsettling, as it was for Salomé, and Nietzsche did little to alleviate her concerns. His reality was a lonely one, and she stood
as a breathtaking possibility. To Salomé, he expressed both aspects simultaneously, which led her to catch sight of the fault
line that Nietzsche's life often treaded. He explained the consequences of his isolation first: "For solitary ones like me, I
must get to know others slowly, even dear ones." But then, in
the same breath, the solitary one gave voice to bold new possibilities: "to be frank, I would like to get you alone as soon
as possible." This was honest, no doubt, but also obsessive and
perhaps a little creepy. At the end of May, in Naumburg,
Nietzsche wrote to Salomé, reminding her of their time
together: "The nightingales sing all night long outside my

window.—In every respect <u>Rée is a better *friend* than I am or can be; note well this distinction between the two of us!</u>— When I'm all alone, I often, very often, say your name aloud— to my very great pleasure!" These were, even for Salomé, forbidden admissions.

By the middle of summer, in Leipzig, the town where Nietzsche had initiated his studies and a philosophical project of self-discovery, Salomé and Rée had begun to make their break with him. He was devastated and, like most devastated men, furious: "Those two persons Rée and Lou," he fumed in August 1883, "aren't fit to lick my boots (forgive this all too masculine image!)." Early commentaries on Nietzsche and Salomé suggest that she was his secretary and disciple, but the letters tell a different story. She was Nietzsche's muse and constant challenge, the force that drove him to contemplate the true meaning of free-spiritedness. But Salomé, in the process, decided to free herself from him. And later she explained that her escape was just in the nick of time.

Nietzsche's sister, Elisabeth, meddled in the relationship, but she was far from the definitive factor in the break between her brother and Salomé. Initially, "the trinity" was to be a monastic order of three free spirits, but Nietzsche quickly came to hate the idea of sharing Salomé with another male companion. "In every conversation between three people," he explains, "one person is superfluous and therefore prevents the depth of the conversation." This was meant to be the justification for disposing of the third wheel, but through the summer of 1882, Salomé began to distance herself not from Rée but from the professor from Basel. In the coming year, he was the one who would be completely abandoned.

As the breakup revealed itself, Nietzsche did what many

desperately lonely people would do—he ran toward it. Hell-
bent, really. If Lou wouldn't have him, he would have to reject
her first. But the deed was done, Salomé escaped with Rée (who
would be her companion for another two years), and Nietzsche
was to satisfy himself only with sour grapes. In the correspon-
dence that precipitated Salomé's departure, Nietzsche wrote:
"Don't write me such letters! What is that kind of wretched
stuff to me? Can't you see: I wish you would raise yourself up
before me so that I need not feel contempt for you." It is possible to understand this contempt as a sign of a deep and lasting
wound, and it probably was, but I now see that it was something else, a sign of a man who couldn't have his way. Nietzsche wanted his relationship with Rée and Salomé "just
so"—monastic and ideal, but also exclusive and intimate, and
always on his terms. He was not one for compromise, and he
had trouble pretending to be something he was not. A relationship often involves lying to the ones we love—speaking half-
truths that suit our beloved. We measure, carefully, what we
say and what we don't. This is part of the game of love, and
Nietzsche was a horrible player. He seemed to say, or write,
everything that entered his mind, and his listeners could take it
or leave it. When Salomé left it, and him, he became furious.

There are echoes of this fury in Zarathustra, in his ravings
against marriage, in his occasional rancor against his interloc-
utors, in his impatience with the mundane affairs of common
courtesy or sanity. A reader is, I think, safe to take Zarathustra's development as a way of understanding the author's
personal turmoil during this time. On September 16, 1882,
Nietzsche wrote: to Salomé, endorsing a theory that she would
later use to interpret his life: "Your idea of reducing philosophical systems to the status of personal records of their authors

is a veritable 'twin brain' idea. In Basel I was teaching the history of ancient philosophy in just this sense, and liked to tell my students: 'This system has been disproved and it is dead; but you cannot disprove the person behind it—the person cannot be killed.'"

There is much that is incisive and much that is wrong-headed about *Thus Spoke Zarathustra*. Its four parts, composed between the years of 1882 and 1885, are the most hotly contested writings in Nietzsche's corpus. Some say they are brilliant. Others, many others, say they are nonsense. But I think one thing is true. Even those who disprove them cannot disprove the person behind the scenes. The contradiction and paradox that one sees in Zarathustra is, to some faint extent, Nietzsche himself. And this, I believe, is no paradox. There is, in the midst of the inconsistency, a brave degree of fidelity between the book and its author, but also, if we're honest, the book and its reader. It maps the divided nature of the modern mind.

In November 1882, when the die had been cast on their love affair, Nietzsche wrote to Salomé, indicating that the contempt he felt for her was but an outgrowth of what he felt for himself: "I had no idea till this year how distrustful I am. Namely, of myself. *My dealings with my fellows have ruined my dealings with myself . . .*" This danger—that companionship could destroy selfhood—is at the core of Zarathustra. Occasionally it appears that this risk, rather than eternal recurrence, is the very essence of the book, but this isn't exactly right. Eternal return is its essence, but it is one constantly threatened by impositions on the self. The self is not a hermetically sealed, unitary actor (Nietzsche knew this well), but its flourishing depends on two things: first, that it can choose its own way to the greatest extent possible, and then, when it fails, that it can embrace the fate that befalls it. Being in love can jeopardize both of these conditions, something that Nietzsche learned with Rée and Salomé. By choice and by circumstance, Nietzsche ended up alone. "To live alone," he writes, "one must be a beast or a god, says Aristotle. Leaving out the third case: one must be both—a philosopher."

In 1894, while Nietzsche rocked in the corner of an insane asylum, Salomé wrote his first biography, arguing that his tragic end was the only one that could have taken place. She insists that "we must direct our attention to the human being and not the theorist in order to find our way in Nietzsche's works. In that sense, our contemplation will not gain a new theoretical world picture but the picture of the human soul in all its greatness and sickliness." For Nietzsche, his philosophical writings and inner life, in Salomé's words, "coalesce completely." His lunacy was not the consequence of a brain tumor, or syphilis, or even manic depression. It was a necessary consequence of his philosophy. To delve too deep into Nietzsche's individualism, skepticism, perfection, and iconoclasm is to flirt with psychological pathology and to run as quickly as possible from the comforts of lasting companionship. This is what a reader discovers in *Zarathustra*.

THE HOTEL WAS SILENT, save for the shuffling of my feet across its red carpet. The doors to the guest rooms of the Waldhaus were paneled in a highly varnished solid oak, crafted by splitting single knotty logs lengthwise and then placing them side by side, making a perfect mirror image—exactly the same, exactly different. Butterflies, clouds, angels, faces passed me in the hall. A moving Rorschach test. An hour later, I caught my breath outside Room 78: two peacocks, facing each other, gave me suspicious glances. I stared them down for a long minute, but then noticed, or rather felt, a gaze at my shoulder. A bald man clad in a gray suit, obviously the night porter, had appeared at the end of the hall. He gave me a steady look, smiled quickly, and then was gone. I was obviously not the first prowler he'd encountered in the hotel.

Five fifty-one. Seven, eight, a dozen more floors in repetition: I picked up speed and began to sweat through my pajamas. Dawn was upon me. I would have to return to the room soon, to make a good showing of living on the surface. I settled into a wicker rocker at the top of the grand marble staircase and closed my eyes for what I thought was just a minute.

Before *Zarathustra* even properly begins, we find him in mid-step. Zarathustra, at the age of thirty, abandons his "home and the lake of his home" and makes for the high peaks to rejoice in the spirit of loneliness. He will aspire to live alone—as beast and god—and be, in Nietzsche's words, a philosopher. But ten years later, in what most people call middle age, he grows weary of his solitary wisdom, "like a bee who has collected too much honey." In other words, he becomes *too* lonely and decides to return to civilization. "Thus did Zarathustra's going down begin." At first, on the descent, he meets no one, but as he gets closer to the valley, in a cluster of trees, Zarathustra finds an old acquaintance, a saint, who sees that the mountain man has changed. Indeed he has. He is lonely now, and not happily so. But Zarathustra provides another, more magnanimous reason for his return: "I love men," he explains. And he continues to search for his beloveds in the town below.

The elision of love and need is a disastrous one for Zarathustra in the early moments of the book. He feigns to love, but in truth, his is a crass need for companions who are fashioned in his own image. Searching for those who will accept his lesson of the Overman just as he has accepted it, Zarathustra reflects a narcissistic desire that must be satisfied in a tightly prescribed way. This is the just-so story of human companionship—one planned out in advance in order to compensate for a sense of psychic or personal privation. The potential lovers and friends that Zarathustra meets in the marketplace, however, do little to fill the void. They are too petty, too stupid, too human.

Zarathustra is not alone in confusing love and need or in experiencing the heartache of this confusion. On some level, a reader realizes that this quest for friendship or communion is fated from the start. Zarathustra seeks impossible companions, at once obsequious and powerful. He needs followers and listeners, but he wants them to be free spirits—in other words, ones who wouldn't deign to follow or listen. When townspeople inevitably fail to measure up, "Zarathustra became sad and said to his heart: 'they do not understand me . . . they look at me and laugh: and as they laugh they even hate me. There is ice in their laughter." And with that, Zarathustra leaves once again for his isolated trails, walking into the darkness, "for he was used to walking at night and liked to look in the face of all that slept." The entire book is a story of a man shuttling between darkness and light, isolation and togetherness.

There is another way of interpreting the "prologue" of *Zarathustra*, another explanation why Zarathustra is unable to

make friends or fall in love. It's so obvious that I'd not even noticed it on my first reading. His isolation has nothing to do
with the deficiencies of his companions and everything to
do with the message he forces them to hear: *God is dead*. This
is an unpleasant discovery, but according to Zarathustra, it
shouldn't come as any huge surprise.

God's been dying for a long time. Our faith in the Divine
has been eroded by a steady onslaught of forces: the advances
in science, the age of reason, the birth of modern capital, the
distraction of consumerism, the deification of the state. God
didn't stand a chance. His death is no cause for celebration; at
best it has created a vacuum that needs to be filled. As Dostoyevsky first remarked, in His absence, anything is permitted; something new can, or must, be done. Zarathustra hopes
that it can be done together by small groups of free spirits. And
it is with this in mind that he extends his teachings of the *Übermensch*, a lesson of self-overcoming. In a post-theological world,
self-overcoming remains one of the few remaining goals. It is
an exciting, terrifying possibility that can place unsustainable
weight on budding relationships.

So what exactly is so frightening about Nietzschean self-
overcoming? Zarathustra explains that it consists in three
"metamorphoses." First, one must become the camel, loaded
down with the baggage of the past, of tradition, of cultural
constraints. This always struck me as the most brutal of the
steps. Usually, when one pictures camels, they are walking in
perfect single file, dutifully carrying their packs. But it's not
always like this. Camels are huge, stubborn creatures—sand
monsters, really—that are not inclined to submit to the strictures that are placed on them. So before the packs are placed
on their backs, they have to be broken. Each camel is staked

to the ground. And starved. If starvation doesn't weaken their will, the beatings commence. This is how one becomes a beast of burden.

But then, Nietzsche writes, in the loneliest desert, a second metamorphosis occurs: "here the spirit becomes a lion who would conquer his freedom and become the master of his own desert." The lion throws off the packs of the camel and, one can only presume, devours its onetime master. This stage appeals to most rebellious—and even some apparently studious— teenagers, and it probably accounts for Zarathustra's popularity in the twentieth century. The lion is the "creation of freedom for oneself and a sacred No even to duty." Such a "sacred No" is the negation of all supposed values, a taking account and a wiping clean. No, this is not violent enough. The lion is the only beast who can fight, and kill, what Zarathustra calls the dragon of the "Thou shalt." This dragon must die so that the will—the sheer individual volition—of the lion can live.

For many—dare I say most—of us, this is as far as we go. We embrace nonconformity and spend our remaining years as the preying lion. According to Nietzsche, there is no great shame in being a lion, and its warring spirit is difficult to maintain and therefore somewhat heroic. Indeed, at the end of the book it remains unclear whether Zarathustra himself has experienced the third and final metamorphosis. There is, however, one thing the lion cannot do and therefore one thing the lion must still become. The lion can wrest itself from duty and burden, but this nay-saying is ill-equipped to create new values. For the sake of new values, the lion must become the child. Herein is the unique value of youth: "A child is innocence . . . a new beginning, a sport, a self-propelling wheel, a first motion, a sacred Yes." The limitation of the lion is that it is still tethered to the ways of the past, even if only to reject them. The child, according to Nietzsche, has the almost miraculous ability to forget and move forward. Which new values will the child create? It scarcely matters, Zarathustra suggests. They will be new—and will look like something you have never seen before. And besides, the question belies a worry that the child doesn't have.

For Nietzsche, for Zarathustra, the value of friendship and romance is to be measured by their ability to facilitate these metamorphoses, to further the cause of the *Übermensch*, to compensate for the death of God. Zarathustra is in search of no average friend or lover. "[I]n your friend you shall love the Overman as your cause," he instructs. The idea that what you love in a person is not a body or a personality, but rather some higher ideal, is a very old one. Aristotle believed that the true friend is the one who is a friend to the highest virtues in another. But Nietzsche's picture of companionship is a hair different: the ideal he pursues in companionship is the Overman, a being who is willing to shake off the trappings of virtue and normalcy for a more liberated future.

Nietzsche had gotten a taste of such a relationship with Lou Salomé. It was enormously invigorating but equally unstable, in part because the stakes were so high. Of course in Nietzsche's day, as in our own, there were ways to overcome this instability, to shore things up in such a way that one could sleep well at night. One way was, and still is, marriage. But Nietzsche worried that this kind of loving friendship, rather than promoting mutual self-overcoming, can slip, slowly but surely, into "love" of a neighbor, meaning one who lives in physical but not spiritual proximity. "You crowd around your neighbor and have fine words for it," Zarathustra accuses. "But I say unto you: your love of the neighbor is your bad love for yourself. You flee to your neighbor from yourself and would like to make a virtue of that: but I see through your *selflessness*."

I ROSE FROM MY ROCKER and glided toward the Bellavista, but before entering, I decided to take one more lap. All the doors were numbered. Except one. I have an almost compulsive urge to open things, so I did. The door swung open and revealed a narrow staircase leading to a short upper hallway. Seven pairs of shoes were set outside three nondescript doors. This was, I imagined, where the staff lived. I turned to leave but noticed a fourth door, Room 301, slightly ajar. The chamber was empty, small and low ceilinged. Against its back wall were more stairs, which led to yet another chamber, what I later learned was the observatory, the highest point of the hotel, and a view. A round of semicircular windows opened out to the mountains, which were just beginning to grant the sun good passage into the valley below. It would be hard to leave now. In the final sentence of *Zarathustra*, Nietzsche writes that he "left his cave, glowing and strong like a morning sun that comes out of dark mountains." This triumphalism was hopeful, wishful, but I knew there were other, more precipitous ways to come down those mountains.

As I learned later, Room 301 is Nino's room. It remains empty. Nino was once the night porter of the hotel. He and Noldi Giamara, the head concierge, were friends of long standing and would often eat together in the observatory. Noldi reflected, "You are very close to the sky up here, you feel like a monarch, but you don't rule over anything. You are close to the place where you work but still very far away, as were the issues that we discussed." Years ago, in late summer, Noldi and Nino went for a hike in the Valchiavenna, a nearby Italian range. They parted ways, and Noldi went ahead so that he could make his barber appointment. "At the trail crossing," Noldi writes, "Nino must have taken the wrong one, the upper path." A storm swept in. The trails were slick. They found the body of the sixty-eight-year-old man the next morning. Sometimes one must be careful not to accidentally take the upper path.

I looked straight down to the valley floor, following it with my eyes as far as I could to the north, to the peaks above St. Moritz. That is where Paul Rée died in 1901. After Nietzsche's death, Rée moved to Sils-Maria and provided medical care for the people of the region. The aging Rée led an apparently saintly existence—some have called it Tolstoyan—selflessly aiding local farmers in the lowlands with the simple tasks of living. It had to be a rather beautiful life. But on October 28 Rée headed for higher ground, making a solo hike around the rim of the Charnadura Gorge, just west of the Julier Pass. No one is exactly sure how he fell. In the days before his death he supposedly told an acquaintance, "I have to philosophize. When I run out of material about which to philosophize, it is best for me to die." To die at the right time: this is what Zarathustra instructs. He knows it's not easy. It frequently involves intentionally choosing the upper path.

I descended the steps carefully, retraced my path to the wicker rocker, and returned to the Bellavista, where my child and dear Kantian peacefully slept.

ON THE
MOUNTAIN

We are, all of us, growing volcanoes that approach the
hour of their eruption; but how near or distant
that is, nobody knows—not even God.

—Friedrich Nietzsche,
The Gay Science, 1882

IN 1885, *ZARATHUSTRA* WAS FINISHED, BUT IN MANY respects it was only the beginning. It was Nietzsche's first attempt, in Walter Kaufmann's words, "to present his whole philosophy. All of his previous works had been stages in his development: with *Zarathustra* the final phase begins." Readers receive an elusive glimpse of the mountaintop, a view that Nietzsche would spend the rest of his life trying to lay open and describe. Upon the publishing of *Beyond Good and Evil* in the fall of 1886, he wrote to his friend Jacob Burckhardt: "Please read this book (although it says the same things as my Zarathustra, but differently, very differently—)." In *Zarathustra* one gets an impressionistic vision of the eternal return and the *Übermensch*. In *Beyond Good and Evil* the symbolism and metaphor are largely gone. It is a systematic philosophical attack on everything that obscures the high peaks where Zarathustra climbs.

Beyond Good and Evil was part of an entrepreneurial experiment: Nietzsche decided to self-publish the book, and he calculated that he would need to sell only 300 copies to make the return on his investment. But just 114 books were sold, with 66 donated to local papers and periodicals. Clearing the mountaintop was going to be a lonely business, and Nietzsche concluded in the disastrous venture that "one simply does not want my literature." He would have to go it alone. By the middle of the twentieth century, however, when Nietzsche studies came into their own, the copies of the book proliferated. One of them was buried in our suitcase under Becca's toys. After breakfast, I dug it out, tucked it in my backpack, promised Carol I would be back before lunch, and left the hotel at a jog.

I FOUND THE TRAILHEAD RIGHT where I'd left it years ago, at the back corner of the Nietzsche-Haus. The trail cut directly uphill, so quickly, in fact, that someone had wisely added stairs in my absence. There is a constant tension when walking on a steep grade. It is best to pace oneself, to let the body adjust to the strenuousness. But I didn't have time for that. I had to be back by lunch. "Sit as little as possible," Nietzsche instructed in 1888, "do not believe any idea that was not born in the open air and of free movement—in which the muscles do not also revel." My muscles could revel later. Gasping for breath in the thin air, I hit the tree line and spiraled toward the ridge where I knew I would at least be able to see, if not reach, the true heights. "Sitting still," my hermit explained, "is the real sin against the Holy Ghost."

For many minutes I heard nothing but the sound of my sneakers on the dirt, but then I began to catch something else on the wind: muffled grunting in the distance, which grew louder, closer, more puzzling, until I realized I was making it. Some things are impossible to suppress in the mountains. This was like being nineteen, but with less oxygen. I slowed for a moment in a shallow depression, a brief stretch of relaxation before the trail made for the next rise. As Nietzsche coursed these trails, he was in search of a philosophy that could have traction in life: "Our first question about the value of a book, of a human being, or a musical composition is: Can they walk?" Can they stand up straight, carry their own weight, cover ground, and make progress? According to Nietzsche, most philosophers, most philosophies, couldn't. I adjusted my pack and reached for the slim book I'd picked up before leaving. Just a short break, then I'd carry on.

Beyond Good and Evil has two primary targets: Kant and women. Kant, one of the great moral theorists of the Western canon, has a theory of duty that drove Nietzsche wild, and not in a good way. The diminutive fellow from Königsberg had a notion of ethical obligation that threatened to abnegate Nietzsche's vision of the free spirit. But there was something more essentially wrong with Kant; even before his ethical theory got off the ground, there was something foundationally amiss in his philosophical system. Before turning to ethics, Kant was an epistemologist: he wanted to know what sorts of truths are available to the human mind. Working in the 1780s, Kant confronted the skepticism of David Hume and the other British empiricists and was intent on overcoming it. Modern skepticism had come very close to reducing the idea of true belief to mere custom, opinion, or habit—that is to say, to not much at all—and Kant wanted to resurrect the primacy of truth and certainty. He did it in a weird and, Nietzsche suggests, philosophically suspicious way.

Kant argued that one apprehends indubitable truths about the world because humans possess a certain mental faculty that can apprehend indubitable truths about the world. His theory is more complex than this, but not much, and Nietzsche argues that Kant spills no small amount of ink on a circular argument. Kant then uses this circular argument to explain where values—moral and aesthetic judgments—come from. Humans' ability to ascertain truth by way of reason makes them special—so special, in fact, that they have "incomparable worth." This means that they cannot be bought or sold or exploited or, in his words, used as a "mere means." It is a good story, but one that begins with a circular (fallacious) argument. None of this would matter, not one bit, if the history of European philosophy hadn't spent more than a century championing Kant's supreme triumph. Writing a century later, Nietzsche had had enough.

Where do moral values come from? According to Nietzsche, it isn't from a shadowy mental faculty that allows a human mind to grasp the truth. Instead, it comes from a basic need, from a fear so pervasive and elemental that modern society has been erected in enduring protest, in the cover-up: the fear of existential uncertainty. I'd never squabbled with Carol about this point, but I had asked, "What attracts you to Kant? You know he's a raging sexist, right?" Yes, she knew. She just didn't care. He provided what she called "manifest certainty," and this made everything else somehow forgivable. Manifest—like clear, apparent, obvious, palpable, definite, self-evident. That kind of certainty. She didn't even care about the argument that much, just the conclusion: every human being had incomparable worth owing to his or her rational faculties, and this meant that no one was any better than her neighbor when it came to the calculus of moral judgments.

Kant's circular argument promised a sort of brute equality that Carol could, and would continue to, live with. I knew her well enough not to argue about this. She'd grown up in a small town in Saskatchewan, far removed from the ivory tower. Her first job at fourteen was waitressing at the truck stop she could see from her bedroom window. The idea that everyone was equal by virtue of their powers of reason was an axiom that didn't have to be proved in an academic way. It had an unquestionable, *practical* power, a belief that led her out of the truck stop and came to buttress the Canadian egalitarianism that had enabled much of her life. To deny its validity was to deny what she'd become: a college graduate, a doctoral student who became a female tenured professor in the discipline of philosophy. Carol defended Kant's manifest certainty as if her life depended on it, because, on a certain level, it did.

Nietzsche explains that for all of philosophy's high-mindedness, it often boils down to satisfying certain brute needs—a desire for protection, an adaptive proclivity for nourishment, a means of effectively negotiating a dangerous world. This is the origin of what he calls "the will to truth," a force that drove Kant to develop a system that came to dominate Western philosophy. Nietzsche suggests that the "greater part of conscious thinking must be counted among the *instinctive* functions, and it is so even in the case of philosophical thinking . . ." One's attraction to manifest certainty is not the outcome of reasonable argumentation but rather the outgrowth of primal fear.

I was on the move again. Christ, it was a long way to the bottom. Absolute certainty did not live up here. The trail narrowed, and the dirt under my feet became lightly treaded rock. To my left was a granite wall that rose indefinitely above; to my right was nothingness that sank indefinitely below. There were no railings or safety nets. After his tirade against Kant, Nietzsche turns to the possibility of walking as a "free spirit." What will these liberated thinkers look like? One thing is sure, Nietzsche contended: "they will not be dogmatists. It must be contrary to their pride," he explained, "and also contrary to their taste, that their truth should still be truth for every one . . . 'My opinion is MY opinion: another person has not easily a right to it'—such a philosopher of the future will say, perhaps."

Nietzsche heralds a coming age of new philosophers, what he calls the "philosophers of the future." Perhaps they will also be moved by the will to truth, but these new thinkers will neither pursue it rabidly as their guiding ideal or, even more dangerous, confuse truth with grand illusion. Kant's "manifest certainty" is worthy of contempt, according to Nietzsche, because it postures as objectivity, a weak argument done up to the nines and presented as absolute truth. At the end of the section "On the Free Spirits," Nietzsche shifts the discourse away from truth entirely. His philosophers will write on behalf of the will to life, or more famously, the will to power. Power is different from feigned truth. Very different.

The sun was almost directly overhead. I'd promised Carol I'd be back before lunch, and we took such promises very seriously. I gave the mountains—Piz Tremoggia and Piz Fora, both at eleven thousand feet—a wistful glance and turned back to Sils-Maria. I could make it by lunch if I ran. Running downhill is a form of controlled free fall. Over the years, I've not perfected it, but I've come to enjoy it. Ideally, you let your legs go in short, light strides and, defying your natural timidity, lean down the hill. Many good runners say that it is not unlike dancing: shoulders loose, arms flapping in the breeze. Above all, don't put on the brakes. Stopping suddenly is the best way to break something. At the end of his speech on the philosophers of the future, Nietzsche rushes down in an unstoppable, never-ending sentence:

> Having been at home, or at least guests, in many
> realms of the spirit, having escaped again and
> again from the gloomy, agreeable nooks in which
> preferences and prejudices, youth, origin, the
> accident of men and books, or even the weariness of
> travel seemed to confine us, full of malice against
> the seductions of dependency which he concealed
> in honours, money, positions, or exaltation of the
> senses, grateful even for distress and the vicissitudes
> of illness, because they always free us from some
> rule, and its "prejudice," grateful to the God, devil,
> sheep, and worm in us, inquisitive to a fault,

investigators to the point of cruelty, with
unhesitating fingers for the intangible, with teeth
and stomachs for the most indigestible, ready for any
business that requires sagacity and acute senses,
ready for every adventure, owing to an excess of
"free will," with anterior and posterior souls, into
the ultimate intentions of which it is difficult to pry,
with foregrounds and backgrounds to the end of
which no foot may run, hidden ones under the
mantles of light, appropriators, although we
resemble heirs and spendthrifts, arrangers and
collectors from morning till night, misers of our
wealth and our full-crammed drawers, economical
in learning and forgetting, inventive in scheming,
sometimes proud of tables of categories, sometimes
pedants, sometimes night-owls of work even in full
day, yea, if necessary, even scarecrows—and it is
necessary nowadays, that is to say, inasmuch as we
are the born, sworn, jealous friends of SOLITUDE,
of our own profoundest midnight and midday
solitude—such kind of men are we, we free spirits!

I knew I was going to slip; in my beat-up running shoes it
was bound to happen. But by the time I did, I was almost
back to town. The descent had been smooth to that point,
and with the Waldhaus in sight, I'd gotten careless. I was no
longer stepping lightly, but instead pounding toward the fin-
ish line on the wide gravel road that led back to civilization.
My heels, which really weren't supposed to be touching the
ground at all, caught a few loose stones, and I went down.
Rolled down, really. Just a bit of road burn and a slightly

twisted knee. Nothing heroic to endure. I made it back in time for lunch and should have been happy enough to take the afternoon to rest.

"THAT, MY LOVE, is the stupidest book," Carol said, pointing to my copy of *Beyond Good and Evil*.

She wasn't picking a fight, just stating a matter of fact. She grinned and pinched the back of my arm as she passed the table where I was unloading my pack. The table was strewn with crayons and action figures, and I cleared a space for my precious book.

Kant's argument isn't circular, she informed me, it's hy-po-thet-ic-al, spelling it out slowly so I could follow her. It's an if-then argument: *If* one thinks that there is such a thing as objective moral value, *then* it must be grounded in the thing that makes all other value possible, namely our rational capacities. Ordinary things—tables and chairs, coloring books, action figures—have value because someone values them. If no one cared about them, they'd cease to have value. She held up the stuffed animal that was Becca's current favorite. The only reason it'd be wrong to decapitate Bumble, she explained, is because it would freak our daughter out. But next week, when Becca has moved on to a new favorite, we could safely torture the thing without being moral monsters. Humans, according to Kant, aren't like Bumble: thanks to our mental faculties, we're valuable even if no one cares about us. Kant isn't trying to convince someone who doesn't believe in truth or morality. He wants instead to give those who already believe in both a supporting argument. He is addressing a sane, generally moral person—not Nietzsche.

We could talk about this later, but for the time being we had to be parents. Collecting the winter coats and gathering Becca up, we made for the lift at the base of Corvatsch, my one-time "parent mountain." It was a balmy sixty-five degrees in the valley, but it would be below freezing at the summit. This was, I remembered, the place for free spirits to contemplate the forbidden. When I was nineteen, in search of "the parent," I came to confront a crevasse that nearly consumed me. Now I was a father, and I should have assiduously avoided such dangers. Since Nietzsche's death, the mountain has attracted a number of other pilgrims, most recently Alain de Botton, who makes the point, echoing Nietzsche, that breathtaking vistas are reached only through arduous climbs: "Fulfillment is reached by responding wisely to difficulties that could tear one apart. Squeamish spirits may be tempted to pull out the molar at once or come off Piz Corvatsch on the lower slopes. Nietzsche urged us to endure." De Botton is probably right, but enduring parenthood sometimes means taking the cable car to the top, which we did.

Even so, the mountain was still more than a little terrifying, and Becca was initially unenthused. I picked her up so that she could see over the side of the gondola, but she wasn't interested and she buried her eyes into my neck. "It's *too big*," she whispered. I could understand: it did seem larger than I'd remembered, forbidding in a way that I was blind to in my youth. It was very difficult to admit, but I was happy for the company and the excuse to forgo the high trails.

By the summer of 1886, Nietzsche was beginning to welcome visitors, young women mostly, to his hermitage in Sils-Maria. He served as their avuncular tour guide through the rocky philosophical and geological terrain. In truth, his health was failing at this point, and it was only the women that kept him on the trails. Without his companions he would not have been able to walk at all. Meta von Salis, the last member of the esteemed Swiss Marshlins family, a scholar of law and philosophy, a unique aristocrat who cut her hair short, and a staunch advocate of women's rights, became Nietzsche's closest friend. Von Salis single-handedly ingratiated the withdrawn philosopher with the political and intellectual elite of the Engadine. He enjoyed her company and appreciated her efforts to brighten his daily existence. Helen Zimmern, a Jewish woman two years younger than Nietzsche, did one better. She came to Sils-Maria to walk with him, but also to translate his study of Schopenhauer and eventually *Beyond Good and Evil*. The feminist, the Jewess, and Nietzsche: this was a strange trinity, but one wholly more congenial than the one he'd envisioned with Salomé and Rée.

Nevertheless, Nietzsche was ambivalent about the role that his attendants played. He was supposed to be their superior, but in many ways he wasn't. After their walks together, the women could stroll on, but Nietzsche would often convalesce for days. His migraines had returned, and the pain was debilitating. He was, during this time, dreadfully worried about becoming weak and infirm. The young women held him together as best they could, but their presence and assistance may have only highlighted his own delicate constitution. There was, I could imagine, much to hate about his situation. He undoubtedly wanted their companionship and comfort, but such a desire was unbecoming for one who aspired to great heights and lonely trails. It is, I think, best to understand Nietzsche's many comments about women in this context.

Was he a misogynist in *Beyond Good and Evil* and elsewhere? Probably. Sometimes. Nietzsche reflected the chauvinism of his age, and he objected to the idea of fighting for the rights of Woman as a concept, but usually his comments about women reveal confusion, even fear, rather than genuine hatred. That being said, he undoubtedly hated Lou Salomé at moments. "In revenge and love," he writes, "woman is more barbarous than man." And he probably felt no small amount of resentment for his female caretakers at points. But on the whole, I want to think, he was too smart to pass rash judgment on half of the human race, and too reflective not to know, at least in hindsight, that his occasional vitriol was a function of his own insecurities.

There is, however, little space for self-knowledge in the midst of rage. I was, by the end of the afternoon, absolutely fuming. The summit was beautiful and snowcapped, but the cramped gondola was freezing and the press of bodies did nothing to warm the metal box. It forced us to be still, which made things even colder—an aluminum container packed with frozen meat. A large woman from Kentucky tried to wedge herself between Becca and me in order to get a better view of Nietzsche's favorite mountain. Her best friend joined her, flourishing a selfie stick, and the picture-taking commenced. What sort of violence could be exacted with a selfie stick? The question occupied many moments of the descent, and I was deep in thought when a soft, familiar voice pulled me to the surface: "Love, let's get a picture."

It's not that I wanted to harm Carol, or the women from Kentucky. Self-inflicted wounds—these were the ones I wanted to cause. My nineteen-year-old self was still, after all these years, alive and kicking somewhere, desperately wanting to slaughter me or pitch my body into a very dark hole. I smiled for the camera. A grinning domesticated animal. By the time we reached the bottom, the picture would have been posted to Facebook and "liked" dozens of times. I'd be expected to "like" the "likes," and the friendship of sheep would continue unabated. I held Becca close and tried my best not to think about the picture.

Coming here with the family had been a bad idea. Before meeting Carol, I never wanted kids. Not even a little. Some days I still don't. Most of my adult life has been premised on not becoming my own absent dad, and I have silently harbored the hope that I can avoid abandoning Becca or Carol. But this hasn't kept me from occasionally thinking that everyone would be better off if I did.

"Art thou a man entitled to desire a child?" Nietzsche asks in his childlessness. "Art thou the victorious one, the self-conqueror, the ruler of thy passions, the master of thy virtues?" No—not even close. Frustration, selfishness, insecurity—parents are supposed to keep these in check, but in my limited experience, they are precisely the psychic phenomena that are born in child-rearing. My friend Clancy, one of the few father-philosophers I know, and one of Nietzsche's best translators—says that parenting is like breaking rocks, only more grinding. Historically, men have opted out of this drudgery, excusing themselves by pretending that "making a living" was somehow as difficult as raising the kids. Of course, this is a grand farce, a convenient cultural myth that effectively keeps women in the home. As patriarchy declines in the coming century, more men will come to feel the painful truth of parenting—that it is frequently beyond difficult.

Becca leaned into me and pulled at my elbow: "Papa, I have to pee."

"Yes, love, I know. So do I. We'll be there in a minute. Can you hold on?"

"Raising children is an uncertain thing," the pre-Socratic philosopher Democritus tells us. "Success is reached only after a life of battle and worry." This is not the banal platitude that raising children is very hard. It is the more unpleasant claim that one is released from the gut-wrenching tensions of parenthood only in death. In this case, being completely disgusted and wanting to run away might just mean that you are paying attention. In Plato's *Republic*, Socrates comments that the reluctant ruler is the only one who should lead the polis. Governing well is nearly impossible, and those who think it is easy or pleasant end up falling well short of the task. Those who want power often do so for the wrong reasons. This thought gave me no small amount of comfort as I clenched the deepest part of me and gave my forbidden thoughts free rein. Maybe the same went for parenting: only those who fear and tremble in the face of parenthood's nasty responsibilities are fit to shoulder them.

At the bottom of the mountain, I swung Becca onto my hip, held her (too) tight, and bolted for the bathroom. When we finally reached the toilet—after dodging tourists and waiting in line, after fumbling around for the Swiss franc to open the stall—we were both soaked. In my botched attempt to be an adult, I was reduced to an infantile state. Becca just looked up into my darkening face and smiled. "Sorry, Papa," she whispered.

We drove back to town along the lake as a late-afternoon shower arrived in the valley. As it cleared, Becca chattered happily about the snowman we'd made at the top of the mountain, and I remembered Meta von Salis's description of her parting with Nietzsche in the fall of 1887. The two had spent nearly every afternoon together during that summer, and they cared for each other deeply. Their farewell happened right here, on the shores of Silvaplana, on the slopes of Corvatsch, not far from the pyramidal rock of the eternal return. The woman had witnessed Nietzsche's steady decline into depression through the previous year, a psychological malaise that he admitted was "worse than those extreme and violent crises that I often fall victim to." We passed the rock, and I remembered how they parted: "The air had that silvery autumnal tone that Nietzsche liked to call 'otherworldly,'" von Salis wrote. It was a breezy afternoon, and the clouds, as they reflected in the lake, shimmered from shore to shore. Crossing the "bleak stretch of field between the lake and the side of Sils facing it," the man let out a small sigh, in sorrow and relief. "I am widowed and orphaned again," he said.

ON GENEALOGY

And amid the roaring and whistling and shrilling,
the coffin burst and spewed out a thousandfold laughter . . .
it laughed and mocked and roared at me. Then I was
terribly frightened; it threw me to the ground. And I cried
in horror as I have never cried. And my own cry
awakened me—and I came to my senses.

—Friedrich Nietzsche,
Thus Spoke Zarathustra, 1883

AFTER THREE DAYS OF FAMILY EXCURSIONS AROUND the hotel, I managed to carve out a morning to myself. It was daybreak, and I'd already been on the trail for several hours. The sun rose, and I slipped my headlamp off and stowed it in my back pocket. I would eat breakfast and lunch by myself. That's what I told Carol before I left.

The most fearsome part of a trek like this is the beginning, but better this than the tired sadness of the gondola on Corvatsch. This exercise was a way of taking hold of sadness, controlling if not quelling it. I'd done it for many years. But I still didn't know what to expect, or precisely when I'd be back from this hike. I'd not said this to Carol, but my pack was stuffed to the brim, so she must have known. Maybe I would be back by dinner. Maybe not. This time, I would decide. On many levels, I know how lucky I am: most companions would be wholly unwilling to stand close and witness a loved one take a risk. "Stand close and witness" is very different from "stand back and watch." The first connotes a careful vigilance that actually enables risk and, with any luck, growth; the second is the resigned curiosity of a person who no longer truly cares. I was deeply fortunate. Carol remains as Nietzsche often describes himself to his readers: a guide rail next to a torrent, but never a crutch.

I was on the high trail above Val Fex, a glacial valley that leads south to Italy, up an incline to Alp Muot Selvas, a rise of seven thousand feet, which delivers a hiker to the foot of the glaciers. My trail cut down to the valley floor at Fex, a cluster of houses at the end of the road that courses the valley. From there I could follow several ridges back into the mountains. This had been my route to a temporary home of my youth: a giant slab of granite wedged diagonally into the rocky terrain located a mile above Alp Muot Selvas. I'd spent two nights under the rock as a teenager, and I wanted to see if the tomb was still there.

"TO BE IGNORANT OF WHAT OCCURRED before you were born is to remain always a child."

These words, written by Cicero more than two thousand years ago, are a shorthand way of understanding Nietzsche's approach in the *Genealogy of Morals*, published in 1887. Nietzsche never lost his most basic philological sensibility, the awareness that to flourish in the present, one must first come to grips with the distant past. In the history of Western philosophy, ethicists usually seek concrete ideals to ground the good life. Nietzsche's approach to morality eschewed this sort of moralizing; instead, it explores the reasoning behind our ideas about virtue. His *Genealogy* doesn't aim to determine what is good or bad, but rather to explain why we have come to make this moral distinction in the first place, and now almost unconsciously. It is, in this respect, a form of intellectual archaeology.

What does a person, or a people, keep only underground? What is beneath the ideals and values that guide modernity? What is behind the mask? In the twilight of his working life, Nietzsche wanted to find out. The year was not a happy one for the man in his mid-forties. Looking the past in the face, he would explain, is difficult and unpleasant for so many reasons. "Of necessity," he writes in the *Genealogy*, "we remain strangers to ourselves, we understand ourselves not, in ourselves we are bound to be mistaken, for each of us holds good to all eternity the motto, 'Each one is the farthest away from himself'—as far as ourselves are concerned we are not 'knowers.'" Perfect self-knowledge is methodologically impossible—a dog in hot pursuit of his bobbed tail—but Nietzsche's *Genealogy* entreats readers to look back long enough to understand what they might become.

When one looks back, it is not unusual to catch a glimpse of something unsettling. Nietzsche argues that despite all pleasant appearances, the history of the Western world is a silent story of suffering, that underneath the orderliness of modern life is a chronicle of pain that has been assiduously repressed. This is how the story goes: at the birthplace of European civilization, there were two types of people, the masters and the slaves, and hence two different kinds of morality arose.

Master morality, according to Nietzsche, developed by the lords of late antiquity, the Romans and the Greeks, was, by its very nature, straightforward. The "good" for the master is the power to advance, to assert oneself, to make progress. That which is "bad" is the opposite: weak, slow, cowardly, and indirect. Nietzsche gives the masterly or "aristocratic value equation": to be good is to be noble; being noble necessarily means that one is powerful; power is beautiful (although it can also be terrible); and anything beautiful is both happy and loved by God. This equation gives the master a quick and accurate assessment of his or her self-worth. This is what Nietzsche means when he writes that the master "keeps himself in clear view." My students occasionally ask for an example of a master, as, I presume, it is difficult to think of one in contemporary society. I mention Augustus of Primo Porta. The marble statue, discovered in the middle of the nineteenth century outside of Rome, is of Gaius Octavius, who would become Caesar Augustus, the founder of the Roman Empire. Augustus stands just shy of seven feet. If he were flesh and not marble, he'd come in at a muscular two hundred and fifty pounds. Add the breastplate and armor, and you get a figure who is twice the size of most philosophers. Larger than life, but not so large that one couldn't aspire to become him. His right arm outstretched, he gazes calmly, proudly past his hand into a future that is his and his alone. He is barefoot—a function of his near divinity rather than a sign of his poverty. In the iconography of ancient Rome, only mortals had to wear shoes.

"What do you think of him?" I remember asking one of my more polite students.

She squirmed for a minute and then said in a voice that was barely audible, "I think he looks like a jerk." The class roared their agreement.

That Augustus is regarded as a jerk in contemporary Western society is unsurprising, according to Nietzsche. What is surprising is the story of how this came to pass.

In the three hundred years between the death of Augustus and the reign of Constantine in the fourth century, Romans went from worshipping a masterly man-god to venerating an emaciated Jew hung unceremoniously on a cross. Nietzsche's *Genealogy* is meant to give an explanation of this transformation. Of course, there were already history books about how the Roman Empire became the Holy Roman Empire, but Nietzsche wasn't interested in a purely historical account. He wanted to explore the moral and psychological shift that he would come to call the rise of "slave morality."

Slave morality is anything but straightforward. The slave gives the master a steady sidelong glance and lies in wait. In the ancient world, the Jews, according to Nietzsche, were the slaves par excellence. The Old Testament makes it perfectly clear: the Jews were the oppressed, and everyone else their masters. The life of an early Jew was simply the worst. The Assyrians drove metal hooks into their jaws and knives into their eyes before impaling them on stakes. The Romans threw them to the lions, burned them alive, and crucified them. It is in the midst of this torture that slave morality was born. It began with a basic insight about pain—that not all suffering

is created equal. There was the truly unbearable variety—
that is to say, the type that had no cause or explanation. And
then there was the kind of pain that could be endured, even
happily: this was suffering for a cause. All one needed was a
very good story about why one was being tortured.

Slave morality, according to Nietzsche, begins in Jewish
ressentiment, the hatred the Jews harbored for their oppres-
sors. Masters are immune to ressentiment, but slaves transform the pain of their inferiority into a searing contempt for
the powerful. Nietzsche, the therapist and patient, knew that
there is something deeply understandable about the roots of
ressentiment (this is, after all, the man who later admits that he
attacks only those movements and ideas that have succeeded).
But he holds that it needs to be held in some sort of check: "That
lambs dislike predatory birds does not seem strange: only . . .
it gives no ground for blaming these birds of prey for bearing
off little lambs." This is, however, precisely what sheep do:
they blame the eagle for his carnivorous ways. Nietzsche imag-
ines the town meeting of sheep who protest their captivity
by formulating a new ethical order: "[T]hese birds of prey are
evil; and whoever is least like a bird of prey, but rather its opposite, a lamb—would he not be good?" This is the point where
natural values begin to be inverted, the moment when Augustus first becomes "a jerk."

The ruler is deemed "a jerk" when slave morality makes
him accountable, makes him guilty—for his strength, that is—
makes him blameworthy for not humbling himself or feigning
weakness. The master is always free to give up his powers,
to make himself as a lamb, to submit to the docility of the
herd. That he is unwilling to do so is a symptom of his moral
depravity—an arrogance bordering on hubris—which the so-

ciety of slaves can never forgive. Of course, Augustus couldn't have cared less about what his slaves thought of him, but for the slaves themselves, this thought, the ability to pass this new moral judgment, kept them alive.

The triumph of slave morality is, by its very nature, surreptitious and subterranean. It flourishes under pressure. Repression and agony, the engines of ressentiment, only make it stronger and more durable. This is not to say that the lives of the Jews and then later the Christians (who carried slave morality to its apotheosis) were made objectively easier in the discovery of slave morality. They weren't. Indeed, Nietzsche claims that they became intentionally harder, sinisterly tortured, as ressentiment took hold of the slaves. If hardship and suffering were associated with moral rectitude, then excruciating pain was a sure sign of a truly saintly nature. What else, Nietzsche asks, could explain the holy self-sacrifice of the Crucifixion?

Throughout the 1880s Nietzsche experimented with and theorized about what he termed "ascetic ideals." The Crucifixion was motivated by such an ideal, but the hermit (in Greek, the *asketes*) of Sils-Maria was interested in the whole range of self-regulating, ultimately self-destructive behaviors. *Ascetic* comes from the word for "monk," but more directly from *asketikos*, meaning "rigorously self-disciplined." This discipline has a long and storied history in the development of the human race. The man who would write for five hours, hike for three, and then write for another five—this man was fixated by the ascetic ideal. Any strenuous exercise or difficult trek reflects the ascetic. Painting, writing, exercising, studying, parenting: they all involve more than a little self-control. But in 1887, as Nietzsche finished the *Genealogy*, he came to see something important about asceticism when it is first appropriated by and then grows out of control in our age of slave morality. When one's life is completely controlled by powerful masters, the discipline of self-denial gives a slave something to do on his own terms. Indeed, it becomes the one thing a slave accomplishes on his own behalf. The slave has few options at his disposal: he can will nothing and be wholly controlled by his master, or he can set his will in motion in the ongoing process of self-negation. The slave has a choice between nonaction, which would eventually bring about his demise, and action, willful but self-abnegating, which would hasten this eventuality. Nietzsche thinks the decision is all too obvious: humans would rather destroy themselves than embody the passivity of willing nothing at all.

WHEN ONE SPENDS TIME ALONE in the mountains, where the air is thin and pure and the ground is cold and sharp, there is an inclination to make oneself equally perfect: thin, pure, cold, and sharp. And this perfectionism—measuring oneself against the grandeur of the mountains—can make the return to the lowlands, and life with others, difficult. It can also feed the ascetic ideal.

On my previous visit to Switzerland, I'd acquired more than a scar on my ear. I'd also come back with something between an affliction and a disposition that I rarely talk about. It's much like the story of throwing rocks into a chasm on Corvatsch, so usually I just avoid it. But the fact is that as a teenager, hiking behind the Nietzsche-Haus, I came to love fasting even more than mountaineering. In fact, I discovered that the two really aren't that different. Both are the quest for impossible extremes. But with fasting, you don't even have to leave home.

When I finally returned after my first trip to Sils-Maria, my mother met me at the Philadelphia airport and wept at the sight of me. As a boy, I'd been positively fat, as a teenager I'd turned thin and wiry, but now I was beyond gaunt. "I lost some weight," I admitted: twenty-two pounds in nine weeks. Yes, it's possible. To this day, when she hugs me, I can still feel her thin arms calibrating—making sure that I haven't wasted away any further in her absence. Over the last fifty years, folk psychology has concluded that severe anorexia is best explained as a response to a lack of personal control. It's not about waist size or body fat or being sexy or fashionable. At root, it's about self-possession. It's still not supposed to happen to, or be suffered by, men. But it is. More often than one might think. Acute fasting, the type that transcends any vain pursuit of physical beauty, is a test, a trial, an exercise of the will. And once exercised in this way, the will is not easily quieted. Fasting dies hard. I believe that, as with most genuine compulsions, its draw, once experienced, is always felt. And I had felt it first in the hills above Sils-Maria.

Fasting, like hiking, can be a respite in a life that is either too chaotic or too repressive (or both), an attempt to escape the forces of these disempowering extremes. "To eat or not to eat?" is one of the few questions of contemporary life that is still largely self-determined. Do you want a doughnut—or six—a rice cake, a piece of broccoli, a thin oatmeal gruel? Or nothing at all? You and you alone get to decide what sustains you. We sometimes hear that hunger fasts have been "broken," but in my experience this isn't quite right. Fasting is not the sort of thing that can be affected directly by an external force—it is willfully executed and must be willfully discontinued. All of this makes psychological dysfunction sound somewhat heroic, which, for a very long time, I thought wasn't far from the truth.

Why fast? The modern age has ingenious ways of setting our wills to work and constructing persuasive narratives about how this work is actually meaningful. But in the nineteenth century, as Nietzsche came of age, these grand narratives began to ring increasingly hollow. Perhaps devoting yourself to your family or the church or the state—or any convention, for that matter—was just a waste of time. Or, more pointedly, a waste of free will and experience. The routine of modern life felt so scripted and routine that Nietzsche and other European thinkers began to question the reality of free will altogether and, in response, to pursue extreme, sometimes harebrained experiences to break the monotony. Fasting was one of them. Most of these practices were cloaked in the rhetoric of medical necessity (simply radical measures to maintain a sound mind and body), but a handful of writers, the young Nietzsche included, saw through the veneer of good health straight to the core of something even more important: self-mastery.

I know all of this sounds crazy, but not to a Nietzschean. It is in times of plenty, of surplus, that practices of self-depravation such as fasting emerge—"during which," Nietzsche writes, "an impulse learns to cower down and abase itself, but also to *cleanse* itself and become *sharper*." He struggled with eating for most of his life. Struggle: like Proteus and Menelaus, inseparable in combat. "If only I could be the master of my stomach again!" he lamented in middle age. And to reclaim mastery, he went to great lengths—experimenting first with vegetarianism, then with a carnivore diet, then with eating nothing at all. Nietzsche said he was interested in the relationship between food and thought, and he believed that thinking was inextricably tied to eating. I'm sure this was part of it. But only part.

In fasting's long and storied history, self-control, in the form of self-deprivation, prepared the way for spiritual transcendence. Fasting, at least in theory, was a means of orienting the will to something higher or deeper. In a 1923 seminar on Nietzsche's *Zarathustra*, Carl Jung explained that "to fill himself with physical matter would make him heavy . . . He could not fly, he would be fettered to the earth." At a certain point during my first summer with Nietzsche I'd gotten a fleeting sense of Jung's words. I stopped being hungry: the craving, dissatisfaction, fatigue—along with my body—slowly slipped away. I no longer wanted to sleep or eat or even read. I wanted only to walk. I was beyond unhealthy, but I didn't feel it, not at all. This type of self-deprivation was my first addiction—and after all these years I still remember it fondly. In truth, since my summer in the mountains, I've never experienced eating or hunger in the same way.

Of course, all obsessions have their drawbacks. Prolonged fasting consumes so much of your life that you have painfully little to give to anything else. It is the most domineering companion, and every waking moment must be devoted to its satisfaction. When I returned to college after hiking with Nietzsche, I immediately joined the lightweight rowing team— what I thought was a socially acceptable mask for a raging eating disorder inspired by a philosophical–quasi-religious experiment. Rowing was thoroughly Nietzschean: self-expression through repetition, flexibility, speed, and, above all, strength. I loved its perfectionism but eventually quit the team when I cracked a rib on a rowing machine and realized that I really didn't like rowing with others. My teammates weren't taking their lightweightedness seriously enough. I wanted companions, but they were, on so many levels, holding me back. I took a similar approach to my social and romantic life. Acquaintances who knew me during this time tell me that I was thoroughly intolerable. And those are the ones who still speak to me.

SIX MONTHS BEFORE BECCA WAS BORN, I started taking the antidepressant Celexa. The pills didn't "cure" me, but they took the edge off living so that it didn't cut quite so persistently and deeply. I took only a small dose—30 mg—and found that I could still laugh and have sex and be sad. It was a bit like having coffee in the morning—I actually felt more like myself. I also stopped caring quite so much about my ascetic regime. I would just take a few pills until Becca grew into a fully functioning adult. Then I would stop. Around that time, I read a Jonathan Lethem piece in *The New Yorker,* and his fictional account of going off Celexa gave me a pretty good idea about the dangers of withdrawing from my little pink pill: dizziness, nausea, suicidal ideations, lucid dreaming. In the days prior to our Alpine journey, however, I'd either conveniently forgotten, simply assumed I'd be fine, or, more likely, willfully sabotaged myself. I'd continue the medication once we returned home. After all, it was such a modest dose, and I was much healthier now. And when I hiked with Nietzsche the first time, I didn't have any pills.

When I was still a student of nineteen, Dan Conway, my professor and guide in all things Nietzschean, explained the pervasive force of the ascetic ideal. It has been one of the principal drivers of Western civilization, and resistance is largely futile. At the time, I was skeptical or maybe hopeful: surely some people could will themselves beyond its self-negating ways. Dan just shook his head and sent me off to Basel.

He was right: asceticism is a persistent force in the field of human values and quickly appropriates more life-affirming ideals that might challenge it. It is so long-suffering, so patient, it can outlast almost any competitor. The ascetic ideal has time and human nature on its side: as Schopenhauer suggests, we are, at base, suffering creatures, and when this insight comes home to roost at last, the ascetic ideal is there to greet us at the doorway of our misery. "Man, the bravest of animals and the one most accustomed to suffering," Nietzsche writes in the *Genealogy of Morals*, "does not repudiate suffering as such; he desires it, he even seeks it out, provided he is shown a meaning for it, a purpose of suffering . . . and the ascetic ideal offered man meaning!"

After four hours on the trail and no food in my stomach, my legs burned and my head swam. I was dizzier than I'd expected. I just had to make it to the rock, and then I'd rest. It couldn't be more than a couple of hours more, and then I was sure to experience a euphoric return to the heights or depths of my youth. Philosophers, after all, have always thought on their feet. After Aristotle died, in 322 B.C.E., many of his students formed the Peripatetic school, a group of wandering lecturers named after the Greek *peripatetikos* ("walking"). The ancient sages of India and Nepal would stay at home during the rainy season, but as soon as it ended, they too would be in motion, thinking and teaching. The Buddha, Jesus, Augustine, Rousseau, Wordsworth, Coleridge, Emerson, Thoreau, James, Rimbaud—all of them, and many more, were walkers. Thoreau, one of the truly great wanderer-thinkers, writes, "Methinks that the moment my legs begin to move, my thoughts begin to flow." The twentieth-century analytic philosopher Ludwig Wittgenstein often visited his collaborator and friend Bertrand Russell in the early evenings, and Wittgenstein would pace the floor of Russell's apartment for hours, cogitating and ambulating. As the evening grew late, he would tell Russell that he planned to commit suicide when he left, presumably when his feet came to rest. So Russell would urge him to stay, on the move—alive.

And then there is *The Way of a Pilgrim*, that most famous Russian tale of walking, first published in 1884, the year that Nietzsche finished the second part of Zarathustra. It tells the story of a mendicant pilgrim who uses walking not to reach any particular philosophical insight but rather to see God. The book is a manual that provides a method to pray without ceasing. God is not dead for this rover. The anonymous walker recites the Jesus Prayer two thousand times in a day, then six thousand times, then many more. "Lord Jesus Christ, Son of God, have mercy on me, a sinner." But the supposed breakthrough, the point at which things in the story get very strange, is when he hinges this short prayer to walking and breathing. The average person takes ten thousand steps in a day, but if you spend the day walking, it can be closer to forty or fifty thousand. At some point in the repetition, the pilgrim becomes the prayer, or the prayer becomes him. What he is worshipping—something distant and otherworldly—somehow comes home in mid-stride. I'd read this account in college, before my first trip to Sils-Maria, and was immediately hooked. I'd ignored the warnings in the preface that such extreme ascetic practices could lead to what church fathers call *prelest*, literally a "going astray," a dreamlike state in which delusion is interpreted as salvation.

Walking may be one of the most sustaining and refreshing of human activities, but slave morality, hinged to the ascetic ideal, was eventually able to co-opt even this exercise to destructive ends. *The Way of a Pilgrim* may be the story of a man who goes on a great hike and finds God, but it is just as likely the glossy fable of a Christian ascetic whose feet suffered countless injuries for no good reason. Pilgrims, the heroes of Judeo-Christian slave morality, travel hundreds, sometimes thousands of miles in intentionally miserable conditions. The harder the better. The trial is meant to cleanse a person, despite the fact that it probably involves dirty blisters, infected cuts, gangrenous toes, and scars that never go away. In the eleventh century, twelve thousand of these sufferers made their way from Germany to the promised land in Jerusalem. Who knows how many actually made it to their destination? Their last days were spent, I can only imagine, rather horribly for the sake of an ideal that demanded still greater forms of excruciation. That the pilgrim decides how to suffer is, I know, some small comfort, but it often seems painfully small.

IT WAS AFTER NOON, and I slowly, too slowly, approached Alp Muot Selvas. The landscape, I'm sure, was truly glorious. I just didn't notice. Why did my return to the mountains have to feel like dying? I was paying attention to exactly two things: the gnawing in my stomach that radiated as a distinct shiver into my chest and groin, and the clicking in my left ankle, a leftover from one of the more stupid moments of my high school years, when I'd fallen off the roof of a Volkswagen station wagon going twenty miles an hour. The glaciers above Fex were in sight, and I tried to focus on my destination, on how good it would feel to curl up under the granite canopy that had kept me relatively protected on my first trek to this valley, but my ankle wouldn't let me. It was a constant reminder of the possibility that the pain of this journey might be pointless.

Every pilgrim goes in search of sanctuary. For Christian pilgrims, sanctuaries are the tombs of saints—St. Peter and St. Paul in Italy or Jesus's empty crypt in Jerusalem—places where holy figures came to rest. There is something unquestionably lovely and morbid about these walkers. Before leaving their families of origin, the pilgrims would write their wills in order to insure that something small might remain after they were gone. They would take off their shoes, not because they had Augustus's immortal feet but because they had pointedly mortal ones—that is to say, because they wanted to feel the pain of being human. And off they would go. Their lives at home were undoubtedly unpleasant (life in the eleventh century was generally unbearable), so they took it on themselves to take control of their suffering, to own it in a particular way.

Nietzsche thinks there is something heroic in this volition to suffer, but he suspects that the whole story becomes dysfunctional in the mouth of the Christian priest. Instead of a simple and honest explanation—that a very long walk is, in some way, a form of owning up to suffering—the priest gives his pilgrims a story of depravity and restoration. Indeed, many pilgrims were actually criminals, condemned by the Inquisition, for example, to make long trips (self-imposed exiles) for infractions that ranged from killing one's father to stealing a loaf of bread. But the priest goes a step further in his justification for pilgrimage: every walker is a sinner, a fugitive, who can be forgiven only through the purification of pain. Of course, many pilgrims seek sanctuary in order to be healed or to find a cure for a loved one's illness, but the story is essentially the same. Human beings are sick or guilty, or both, and need to suffer their blisters and broken ankles in order to be saved. This remains the exposed backbone of the ascetic ideal.

Days earlier, Carol had offered to join me on this trek, but I had, at least in the early moments of the hike, been glad to be alone. I was no longer glad. I caught sight of an outcropping of loose granite on the southeast side of the valley, a deposit of geometrical boulders that looked like the remnants of an ancient temple. But after twenty more minutes of walking, this impression gave way to another. If this was once an ancient temple, it was the world's largest. The rocks stretched for a half mile. Finding a lone rock in the midst of this high plateau would have been impossible were it not for a single landmark, a small waterfall that had, I presumed, only deepened in my time away. There it was, running along at a good pace, directing any sojourner to a hidden diagonal slab on the edge of the stream that it created. Even in my youth, the Christian imagery of springs and rebirth had not been lost on me, nor was the irony that this was the place where Nietzsche had come to criticize the ascetic ideal.

The rock was a ten-foot-long diamond, two feet thick, cut

roughly in the shape of the state of Maine. How it had come to be lodged in the earth as a perfect cantilever lean-to will remain a mystery, but I have a hunch that it fell and slid from a great height. I'd spent seven hours en route, and now I was here. I should have been much, much more grateful than I was. The best stories of pilgrimage are those that end in a flood of cathartic tears as the sojourner finally approaches the sanctuary and a monk meets him at the threshold to wash his festering feet. There is, in this mythic moment, a transcendental communion in which the lowly searcher and the divine goal become one. But how many pilgrims reach the sanctuary and collapse, how many cry tears of despair in discovering that the sanctuary is, in fact, a grave? We typically don't hear about these pilgrims, but perhaps we should.

I crawled under my rock and, pulling my pack in behind me, bedded down in midday. It was dark and cool and somewhat pleasant, but not transcendental or uplifting. I just wanted to go back. Not back to the Waldhaus, but way back: to a time before these thoughts. Where are the stories of the disaffected pilgrim, the one who never finds what he is looking for? Or the pilgrimages that simply repeat, in caricature, all the heinous futilities of life? I'm sure they occur, more often than one might like to consider. I set my head down on my pack and let the hard ground grind into the crest of my pelvis.

WHEN I ROUSED MYSELF, it was the magic hour, that time of late afternoon just before twilight, when even the most pitiful scene seems to light up from within. My hips throbbed, but a cool breeze swept down from above Alp Muot Selvas and caressed my exposed cheek and ear.

I had awoken with a thought, and now I had a goal: home.

For the famous pilgrims, comfort is sought and found in some distant sanctuary. A cosmic reconciliation is achieved but only by forsaking all others and following the arduous path to God. But maybe even failed pilgrims find a modicum of salvation. After discovering that pain is just pain, that the tomb is completely empty, that a single foot-washing can't scrub away the dirt of human existence, some dejected pilgrims still get to go home. Maybe *this* is salvation. Perhaps the failed pilgrim wants nothing more than a bit of tenderness, an immediate, simple sense that the world isn't completely and utterly hopeless.

In many respects, the second half of a pilgrimage, the trek back to society, is much harder than the first. The fatigue is undoubtedly worse, and the wounds from the first days of the trip are scarcely healed. Abraham famously took his son up Mount Moriah and was willing to sacrifice him to God. That's difficult, but imagine the journey home with Isaac by your side, the boy you were willing to kill. How much harder is this trip? If one makes it back through the guilt, pain, and disappointment, perhaps the home itself, the place of initial departure, has been transformed in the interim. Perhaps, like the biblical Job, after losing everything, it is possible to get everything back again double. How many failed pilgrims have achieved success after the fact, in their return to everyday life? Of course, this is not the stuff of Christian devotion, but perhaps it is better, or the best: the truth. Perhaps a pilgrim triumphs not in hardship but in the rare moment when they learn to accept something soft at home. As I sat under my rock, an otherworldy chuckle, which I still don't understand, escaped me, and I arose.

I made toward my family, walking away from the site of pilgrimage toward what Becca fondly calls "softing." One doesn't have to go anywhere to experience softing. Softing is usually performed with the back of a hand or, if you're Becca, her nose. It is the softest of strokes. Softing can't be done at a distance. It usually takes place in the early mornings or late at night, almost every day, preferably with all the members of her family, in bed. One can soft spontaneously or ask to be softed, and the request is always granted. In the midst of softing, uncontrollable laughter is not only permitted but expected. It is the opposite of hardship. These are love's true conditions.

DECADENCE
AND DISGUST

To choose instinctively what is harmful to oneself . . .
is virtually the formula for decadence.

—Friedrich Nietzsche,
Twilight of the Idols, 1888

F OR A MAN WITH NIETZSCHE'S GENERAL CONSTITU-
tion, psychological uplift was a suspicious sign—good
weather before the flood. After battling with poor health and
the ascetic ideal in 1887, concluding that the grip of both was
tight and enduring, he seemed to suddenly wrest and regain
himself. The spring of 1887 had been miserable. He had traveled to Nice, which was a monstrous mistake. The bright lights
and clatter of the seaside town had driven the philosopher to

distraction, so in the following year he decided to spend his months away from Sils-Maria in Turin. In the city itself, at last, he found requited love.

Turin was hospitable to Nietzsche's particular physiological needs. Here, the sun seems to cast long, warm shadows from dawn to dusk. In the early morning a walker can traverse the city by way of narrow cobbled streets without encountering a passerby. The streets go on forever, until they don't, when they open into vast squares that appear to draw sunlight and people in exactly the correct proportion. Nothing is rushed or hasty. Things happen "in good time" rather than "on time." With the Alps in clear view, the inhabitants of Turin live and work by nature, rather than apart from it. In April 1888 Nietzsche wrote, "Turin, my dear friend, is a capital discovery . . . I am in a good mood here and work non-stop. I am eating like a demigod, [and] I can sleep . . . It's the air that does it, energizing, dry, jolly." He was accustomed to surviving in, perhaps by virtue of, the nowhere of Sils-Maria, but here in Turin he found what he called "the first place where I am possible!" Possibility is usually regarded as something discrete: a particular opportunity that can be realized. But as Nietzsche found out in Turin, possibility can mean so much more.

In May, Nietzsche's mood swelled: "A charming, light, frivolous wind in which the heaviest thoughts take wing blows on good days." In Turin the aging man could feel the grand extravagance of possibility. Gravity no longer gripped him in the same way, and he could relish, perhaps for the first time, the music of his day. It wasn't Wagner's—this was the music of Nietzsche's past. It was Beethoven's Ninth and, above all, *Carmen*, to which the philosopher was drawn. I'd never understood the attraction. On the edge of my twenties, I thought that the opera's appeal had more to do with the composer than with the plot (Bizet, like Nietzsche, died well before his popularity was secure). But now, closing in on my forties, I began to understand Nietzsche's appreciation for the libretto and score.

Carmen is a light treatment of something absolutely dark, the terrible destiny of star-crossed love. Carmen first seduces, then spurns, and finally destroys Don José, who, in turn, loves her and stabs her to death. This is not the Passion Play that presents the suffering and death of a soon-to-be-risen Christ; it's just a passionate, gorgeous play about average people who kill each other. *Carmen* and the *Ring* cycle may have certain events in common (murderous and lustful ones), but Bizet's touch is entirely different. *Carmen* is sensual, far from the asceticism that had taken over much of Europe. In Bizet's beautiful figure, there's no self-restraint, no second-guessing, no transcendental pretenses, just the headlong and joyous rush to the end. Nietzsche regarded the opera as a palliative for a culture in the throes of a particular sickness that he would call "decadence."

The term doesn't appear in Nietzsche's writings until 1888, but a closely related one had emerged in 1883, in the year of Wagner's death: *Entartung*, meaning "degeneration." Despite the central role that decadence plays in his later works, Nietzsche never gives it a detailed treatment. It is present, always present, but, like many pervasive forces, ill-defined. It is easy to think that Nietzsche was a straightforward opponent of decadence, but it is also easy to be wrong. In 1888, as his health improved, Nietzsche took account of the spiritual illness that plagued all the inhabitants of Western modernity, himself most of all. It is impossible to assess the extent of a disease while one is suffering; only in respite—a temporary reprieve from one's fate—can the scope of a serious ailment be properly understood. In Turin, Nietzsche finally saw that "Nothing has preoccupied me more profoundly than the problem of *decadence*." This isn't just the realization of a thinker who suddenly discovers that his philosophy has been about an unspoken topic; it's the admission of a man who has finally uncovered the underlying ethos of his life.

Nietzsche himself was a decadent, a product of his age and its *haute bourgeois* culture. He was coddled by his mother as a child, by his sister in young adulthood, and by his protectresses in later life. He never worked—at least not in the sense of dirtying his hands—and for many years of his adulthood he lived on an academic pension and the charity of wealthy friends. The Nietzsche-Haus was, I grant, a grocery store and boardinghouse while he stayed there, but it was nice enough. He was a man of letters and languages, a person who could truly understand the words of the English philosopher Thomas Hobbes: "leisure is the mother of philosophy." Yes, there was hardship, but it was often the self-imposed variety. In a letter to his friend and caretaker Malwida von Meysenbug, he writes of the close quarters he's shared with decadence: "I am, in questions of decadence, the highest authority on earth."

Decadent meals, decadent facades, decadent upholstery, decadent music—taken at face value, they are various signs of great wealth. But Nietzsche believes that these extravagances mask sickness and decay. The desire for a decadent meal, one meted out carefully over the course of hours, is a symptom of degeneracy, of one who cannot easily stomach normal food. A building needs a facade only when the supporting structure is ugly. Gaudy upholstery usually covers disproportionate furniture (who would think of covering a Shaker bench?) and is made for overly sensitive backs. Decadent music, bombastic and saccharine, is written for ears that have trouble hearing. Decadence arises out of weakness, as a shroud that covers a frailty on the brink of self-destruction, and in the cover-up, it quickens decay by allowing it to quietly fester and spread. It is life's last, overdone flourish, a harbinger of death.

In 1888 Nietzsche tried to come to terms with the gratuitous decline of the fin de siècle, but also, more personally, with the decline of the individuals who lived in its twilight. He wasn't the first to do so. Dostoyevsky's *Notes from Underground*, published in 1864, opens with a narrator's stark admission, one that Nietzsche would echo in the treatment of his own decadence: "I am a sick man. I am a spiteful man. I am an unattractive man. I think my liver is diseased. But I know nothing of my disease or precisely that which ails me." Nietzsche, like Dostoyevsky's character, had an intimate knowledge of decay. There is no "outside" to a decadent life, no privileged view from which to diagnose one's own illness or witness one's own death. But one can surely try, and Nietzsche did just that through the last productive years of his life. During his final year in Turin he wrote with the frenzy of a dying man, five books in a year: *The Case of Wagner*, *Twilight of the Idols*, *The Antichrist*, *Ecce Homo*, and *Nietzsche Contra Wagner*. All of them were, in some sense, autobiographical, and together they represent a physician-philosopher's attempt to get a hold of himself. Time was of the essence.

From whence did Nietzsche's illness spring? Confronting the problem of decadence was, for him, to face once again the figure whom he regarded as the arch-decadent: his "father," Richard Wagner. Wagner had controlled many of the philosopher's formative years and had served as the parent he never had. At the end of his life, Nietzsche wanted to take account of what exactly had been passed—a legacy, an infection—from father to son. A decade after his break from Wagner, Nietzsche finally attempted to explain it. In 1888, looking back, he wrote, "It was, in fact, high time to take farewell then [in 1876]: soon enough I got proof of that. Richard Wagner, apparently the most triumphal, while in truth become a decayed, despairing *décadent*, sank down suddenly, helpless and disjointed . . ." The contagion of decadence, however, had already been passed down to his progeny.

AFTER A DAY UNDER MY ROCK high in the Val Fex, I'd returned to the Waldhaus and happily discovered, to my half surprise, that Carol and Becca were still there. The softness of their welcome had been a great relief, and I convalesced for several days, enjoying the amenities of a decadent world.

My father, Jan, would have adored the world of Das Waldhaus Sils, especially its library, which was fully stocked with beautiful literature, books that struck me as there to be admired but not necessarily read. He loved these types of places: gorgeous rooms filled with the trappings of culture, set off from the rest of society. The actual philosophy and literature, however, would have been beside the point; the look of the books would have been enough for him. There were first editions of Mann, Hesse, and Jung interspersed with glorious coffee-table books of the landscape and the painters who worshipped it—all of them under glass, but not under lock and key.

A couple of days after my arduous solo hike I tried the glass doors and they popped open. In this sort of library, one could read but not too quickly, not for the sake of extracting a specific point. The task of reading in a room like this is subtle and complex: it involves the ability to complement and accentuate the decor, to be seen perusing the right books in the right way, to enjoy being out in the world reading. It is not unlike eating by oneself in public, which Nietzsche did routinely. The self-consciousness was palpable. In the corner of the library, alone against the ubiquitous oak that adorned what now seemed to be every wall, hung a nondescript frame. In the middle of the frame, in black and white, from the neck up, was a forty-year-old Nietzsche. Somehow the iconoclast had been turned into tasteful decoration or, even more stunning, an icon.

I glanced up from my book, Theodor Adorno's *Dialectic of Enlightenment*, and gave the image on the wall what I hoped was a long, pensive look. It was a famous shot of the philosopher. This was a reproduction: a Nietzsche deep in thought, staring off into the distance. He looked impeccable, mustache trimmed and combed, hair coiffed, eyes piercing. This too was obviously staged.

Most icons present the portrait of a saint or Christ or the Holy Mother. They face a viewer squarely and hold a stare with both eyes. Nietzsche was different. This was an icon given in profile, who had no interest in making eye contact with anyone. He was only partially there—half of his face permanently masked, visible only to the other side of the world. I'd tried in vain to get his attention for a few minutes, eventually giving up and making my way to the *Halle* of the Waldhaus at a leisurely pace: I had a meeting to keep.

Lining the corridor were tasteful display cases filled with pictures of the mountaineers who had been visiting the region for more than a century. Fit and dapper, they posed on escarpments and narrow trails, high above the villages where they had, I imagined, left their families behind. "The individual," Nietzsche writes, "has always struggled to keep from being overwhelmed by the group. If you try it, you will be lonely often, and sometimes frightened." These men did not look frightened. Striving, yearning perhaps, but not frightened. They were happy to be away. Nietzsche explains that "no price is too high for the privilege of owning yourself." The photographs were grainy and small, so every climber looked exactly like my father. I sometimes forget who he was and what he looked like, but then I see him, faintly, everywhere.

The lobbies of many modern hotels try, unsuccessfully, to compress multiple functions into a room that is altogether too small. It functions as a sitting area, a place to check in, a place to do business, a place to sit at the bar, a place to serve yourself coffee, a place to walk through with your children, a place to buy toothpaste, a place to pick up pizza and take it back to your room. The Waldhaus does not have one of these lobbies. Instead, at its foyer is a small room with a concierge desk, behind which stands a wall of cubbies that hold two large key fobs per room. There is no sitting or toothpaste-buying here. There also isn't any talk of money or bills (that is done in a separate, sound-proofed room to the right of the front doors). The vestibule of the hotel has exactly two purposes: it is a locus of welcome and a point of departure—a gateway, where one spends just a moment. It was large enough to appreciate the threshold between past and future, and not large enough to do anything else. I passed through and, in a moment, was into the heart of the hotel again.

In the Waldhaus, if one wants to sit and have coffee, tea, or anything, there is a specific place for that, just beyond the entry. It is a massive sitting room. There is no buffet, and guests never serve themselves. This is the *Halle*. It's what I always imagined a drawing room would look like, but far grander. From its thirty-foot ceiling hang a dozen crystal chandeliers. They would be gaudy anywhere else. The floor is wood, but it is so smooth and solid it feels like concrete or terrazzo and is covered by a variety of Oriental rugs. These rugs, more than a dozen of them, puzzled me at first. Each one was about the size that would fit in a small family room in the States. Why hadn't they just bought one large rug and been done with it? Because—in the words of Urs Kienberger, the Waldhaus "innkeeper," who now approached me at a deliberate stroll—it would be a pity if everything had to be practical.

As we shook hands and walked the length of the *Halle* toward the windows, the rugs made more sense. They created separate but permeable spaces—virtual living rooms where couches and chairs were arranged for groups of four and five. Occasionally a small rug and a single love seat would be tucked into a corner behind the drapes that adorned the expansive windows, creating a place for those who preferred more intimate quarters.

"Is this all right?" Kienberger gestured to a grouping of blue high-back chairs and explained that they were the same age as the hotel itself. "I have a predilection for the old," he admitted as we took a seat. A whip-thin server—"waitress" seems too informal—her hair pulled back tightly, appeared, took our order, disappeared, and appeared again with coffee.

Perhaps she was nice-looking, maybe even pointedly attractive, but her uniform—beige slacks, vest, white shirt, bow tie—made it impossible to tell. What is certain is that she did her part in making our trip as effortless as possible. By the end of our stay, she knew Carol and me by our (last) names, knew our drink orders, what we liked in our coffee, what room we were staying in: Waldhaus guests aren't to be bothered with unnecessary questions or bills. It was like having a butler in a grand house. For Kienberger, she *was* a butler in his grand house. And he had guests.

He couldn't talk for too long, he began. It wasn't that he didn't want to, but it wouldn't be fair to the other visitors of the hotel. The job of an innkeeper is to make all his guests feel equally welcome, and this depends on divvying up one's time fairly between patrons. It was, he admitted, a matter of keeping up appearances, but in the *Halle*, this was rather important. After dispensing with pleasantries, he dove straight into my interest—the philosophers who had called the Waldhaus home. Perhaps he saw the *Dialectic of Enlightenment* in my hand, perhaps it was already on his mind, but Kienberger leaned in to share a hotel secret: "Adorno stayed here for four hundred and twenty days."

I wasn't altogether surprised. For Adorno, the Waldhaus would have evoked intense love and disgust in equal parts. In any event, he would have been thoroughly fixated. Theodor Adorno, one of the founders of the Frankfurt School, was Europe's leading social critic for much of the twentieth century, and he was Nietzsche's self-proclaimed philosophical heir in Europe. Born in Frankfurt in 1903 to a wealthy Jewish wine merchant and an opera singer, the young Adorno was no stranger to modern decadence, and as he aged, the relationship between the two thinkers only deepened and became more complex.

Like Nietzsche, Adorno was a polymath, specializing in music, philosophy, sociology, and psychology. These were the instruments he would come to use to diagnose and treat Western culture. In 1929, after completing his degree under Paul Tillich, the author of *The Courage to Be*, Adorno began to theorize where Nietzsche had left off in *Twilight of the Idols*, attempting to answer a series of very difficult questions: What are the possibilities for human existence in an age that seems intent on destroying itself? What retards its power and limits its reach? What hastens decadence? How can a culture or a person overcome the decline that appears almost destined to occur? Adorno sought his answers at the Waldhaus.

Within the Frankfurt School, Adorno joined Max Horkheimer, Walter Benjamin, and Herbert Marcuse in espousing what has come to be known as "critical theory." It was, at least at first, a neo-Marxist movement, one that held that culture itself could be, and was being, used as a force of oppression. This might seem like a stretch. Culture—entertainment, consumerism, the arts—doesn't seem like the sort of thing that can imprison a people. This intuition, however, Adorno argues, is precisely the thought that lowers one's defenses. Popular culture shapes a people's preferences, delimiting the scope of human activity and desire. Our consumer culture might give us choices, might give us the semblance of being free to choose, but this liberty amounts to pitifully little if everyone is given the same circumscribed options. Critical theory, according to Horkheimer, who coauthored the *Dialectic of Enlightenment* with Adorno, was meant to free people from the subtle forces that enslaved them. How it was supposed to do that had, during my years as a graduate student, completely eluded me. But the Waldhaus gave me some idea.

The critical theorists—following Nietzsche—attacked *popular* culture in all its forms. They objected to the commodification of beauty and the sublime and the leveling out of difference and individual taste. Like Nietzsche, Adorno both abhorred and was riveted by herd mentality. Unlike many psychologists, Adorno asserted that this mentality wasn't a natural social impulse but a grand performance orchestrated by a priestly master (he came of age in Nazi Germany and wrote against fascism in all its forms). The sheep that comprised the herd could, at any time, opt out of the performance, but the theatrics of culture combined with the necessities of capitalism had given it an almost irresistible draw. Still, Adorno wrote in 1951, "If they would stop to reason for a second, the whole performance would go to pieces, and they would be left to panic."

I looked over Kienberger's shoulder, across the graceful space of the *Halle*. This was no place for the herd. We'd spent the last ten minutes discussing Adorno's vexed relationship with the hotel in light of his later philosophy. On a nearby rug, a small group of well-dressed Germans were analyzing the nuances of Bach's Mass in B Minor. At the entrance to this grand lounge, a couple in their mid-sixties discussed Hölderlin's poetry in hushed but audible tones. One way of retreating from pop culture is to embrace unabashed elitism. This was culture—exclusive, but not oppressive. Adorno was drawn to it. He liked the glacially paced meals with intelligent companions, the elegance that gave way seamlessly to natural beauty, and, above all, the quiet. Quiet: the one thing the herd cannot abide. Silence, the sound of oneself, enables—even necessitates—thinking. When Adorno suggests that a mindless follower "stop to reason for a second," he intends this to be, I can only assume, in silence. There are quieter places in Sils-Maria, such as the ten-by-twelve bedroom where Nietzsche summered, but there is a welcome hush that still pervades the Waldhaus.

My time was almost up. Kienberger had other guests to attend to. As he rose, almost on cue, the music began at the far end of the *Halle*. "Adorno loved the hotel," he repeated, turning to go, "but he hated *that*. He despised the trio." The Waldhaus trio was an establishment as old as the hotel itself, and I'd heard that the playlist had not changed in generations. The violin and bass swelled a bit and drowned out the possibility of communicating in whispers. I thanked him, perhaps too loudly, and he was gone.

The music broke the silence, I thought, but it wasn't really that bad. A variation of Pachelbel's Canon in D slid into Brahms, which somehow morphed into Mozart. It was chamber music for beginners, the classical top forty: a little syrupy at points, but not at all unpleasant. God, Adorno must have been such a snob, I thought. But then it began: show tunes, lots of them. I got up to leave, but it was too late. The prelude to *Annie* had begun. Becca would have loved this. The trio played it in high style, trying to mask it with additional stanzas and improvisation, but there it was, as clear as day: "Tomorrow." Nietzsche and Adorno would not have contained their revulsion.

As I left, I passed the glistening Welte-Mignon in a blue room that separated the *Halle* from the dining room. It was a player piano, but not just any player piano. The Welte-Mignon company had produced its first keyboardless reproducing pianos in 1905, and this was one of them. It was basically the world's first stereo. A cabinet full of piano rolls, the perforated scrolls that one would have to insert into the machine to make it play, stood nearby. I looked inside. "The Golden Age": Adorno must have loathed that one too, played night after night in deadly repetition.

The advent of this "piano's" forward-looking technology was the death knell of real music. For a moment, as I passed, I thought about Walter Benjamin, arguably Adorno's closest friend, who had written "The Work of Art in the Age of Mechanical Reproduction" in 1936. Benjamin was writing about film, but the point held for the tunes of the Welte-Mignon: "Even the most perfect reproduction of a work of art is lacking in one element: its presence in time and space, its unique existence at the place where it happens to be. This unique existence of the work of art determined the history to which it was subject throughout the time of its existence." Presence— that is what the Waldhaus had promised: the "luxury of space," to use Kienberger's words. Presence connotes a particular place and time where something, perhaps something significant or singular, could be done. But that was impossible even here. The unique existence of anything—what Nietzsche had searched for his entire life—was nowhere to be found. Just repetition, complicity, and frustration.

IT WAS ALMOST DINNERTIME. I'd have to put on my suit soon. As I turned to the Bellavista, I glanced out the front entrance. A light yellow Porsche 911 pulled into the driveway—

maybe forty years old, solidly vintage, but in immaculate condition. A 911 had been my father's first car. His doting grandmother bought it secondhand for "Rocky," her only grandson, before he turned sixteen. It had been repainted light yellow, thick and glossy. Rocky drove it, like most things, very hard. My mother met him and his Porsche in their hill-climbing days. Who could make it to the top first? That was always the question. Fast and dangerous, car racing was supposed to be the proof of muscularity in car and driver. But glossy paint can, and often does, conceal deep imperfections.

If you redline a car in third gear, miss the upshift into fourth, and instead *downshift* to second—a driver can "drop a valve." When this happens, the fragile stem of the engine valve breaks off under pressure and gets pulverized in the piston cylinder, alerting a cautious driver that he should pull off and get the car fixed immediately. Jan was the opposite of cautious and didn't pull over; instead, he tried to race the broken car home to Reading, Pennsylvania. It was only twenty miles as the crow flew. The engine seized up at the city limits. Death precipitated by decadence. Jan lived and died in a similar fashion.

When I was ten years old, on a rare visit to my father's apartment in New York, he took my brother and me to Delmonico's, a famous restaurant, at 56 Beaver Street. He had three martinis, a giant bowl of mussels, and a Baked Alaska. "Brought these from Pompeii," he said on our way out, pointing to the marble pillars at the entrance. I didn't know what Pompeii was until many years later, but I do now. Ten years after our dinner, I heard from my mother that at one point he'd either fallen or jumped from a great height when he was drunk, shattering his jaw and teeth. He almost died. Ten years after that, my brother and I met him in New York, outside of Memorial Sloan

Kettering, where he'd just been diagnosed with late-stage esophageal cancer. We went to a little hole-in-the-wall for dinner. He wasn't hungry, but he made a great show of it. Slurping, choking, coughing his way through the broth at the bottom of a bowl of mussels.

That night at the Waldhaus, dining with Carol and Becca, everything tasted slightly off. Maybe it was the white tablecloths of the dining room, or the image of my daughter— back straight, elbows off the table, dressed in her finery—or the overwhelming number of silver implements spread around my plate, or the aroma of roasting flesh from the kitchen, or the definite urge to vomit, or the faint hint of self-loathing, or the translucent sauce at the bottom of my soup bowl— whatever it was, I couldn't escape the smell of mussels and broth.

THE ABYSMAL
HOTEL

*We are unknown to ourselves, we men of knowledge—and
with good reason. We have never sought ourselves—how
could it happen that we should ever find ourselves?*

—Friedrich Nietzsche,
On the Genealogy of Morals, 1887

DURING HIS MOVE FROM SILS-MARIA TO TURIN AT
the end of 1888, Nietzsche reflected, or admitted or lamented: "I am a decadent." But apart from this, he maintained,
"I am also the opposite. My proof for this is, among other
things, that I have always instinctively chosen the right means
against wretched states; while the decadent typically chooses
means that are disadvantageous to him." To call Nietzsche a
decadent seems strange, but he understood that to be decadent

was simply to be in the last stages of decline. And he was. Nietz-sche knew that he was sick, and he took drastic measures, first in Sils-Maria and then in Italy, to counteract its effects. Decline was inevitable, but how one went out was decidedly not.

Sils-Maria would remain in Nietzsche's memory as a place to work through the temptations of decadence. At the time, the boardinghouse where he stayed was owned by the Durisch family. It wasn't the "Nietzsche-Haus" then, just a house where an old professor would routinely summer. Nietzsche came and went largely unnoticed and undisturbed by the inhabitants of the village. He had brought hundreds of books to his small bed-room in the summer of 1883. At least he had a bit of company. Many nights, when the landlord went to sleep, Nietzsche would sit alone in the quiet darkness of an empty house. He admitted that the austerity and loneliness of his bedroom, with its ceil-ing that one could easily touch without stretching, was often a difficult kind of confinement. In "the evenings, when I sit all alone in the narrow, low little room [I find it] tough going" he wrote to one of his few friends. It was, however, a calculated type of "tough going," an ascetic regimen without the promise of a flowery afterlife, one that was simply supposed to make him stronger, and perhaps delay the onset of collapse.

With this in mind, after my evening with the memory of my father's mussels and the Welte-Mignon at the Waldhaus, I decided to return to the Nietzsche-Haus. When I'd first visited as a very young man, I could still get the sense of Nietzsche's struggle with decadence. Exhaustion was unavoidable, but if one had the courage, one could choose to burn quickly, or even more quickly—that is to say, brightly. Maybe something of that remained.

There had been nothing fancy about the house in the late

1990s, nothing to distract a person from himself or the task at hand. It had been open to the public only since the 1960s, but it was still largely out of the way. It was public *and* private, an appropriate symbol of the bifurcation Zarathustra had embodied as he shuttled up and down the mountains of existentialism. It had seemed possible to explore the bestial here, the genuinely Dionysian, in peace. At that point the landlord of the Nietzsche-Haus owned a giant wolfhound named Merlin. Merlin was selectively friendly—in other words, terrifying. "He likes you," said the landlord upon meeting my nineteen-year-old self for the first time. Merlin sniffed my crotch. At night, the dog was perfectly silent, but I was left to imagine that he was still there, somewhere, in the darkness. When I wandered the short, empty hallway of the house late at night, I half hoped that we would meet. We never did.

Nietzsche's room wasn't always locked in those days. I'd checked. It looked and smelled pretty much like my room across the hallway. An almost mirror image. This was where great thoughts, great creations, had taken place. I would stay here for a little while. I knew, even at the time, that this was ridiculous: these walls also had witnessed great aspiration, bordering on pathetic delusion. "I am no man. I am dynamite"— this was the place where this thought first arose. Dynamite from the Greek *dunamis*, meaning "power." How could one become dynamite, become the will to power? The point of art, according to Adorno, is to bring chaos to order. How much chaos could even the smallest bit of dynamite create? I spent most of my first trip to Sils-Maria trying to find out.

The short hall had always been empty. I was left alone with the pictures on the walls—the smudged photographed skulls of Gerhard Richter. Hamlet sees the skull of Yorick and says it best: "Alas, poor Yorick! I knew him, Horatio; a fellow of infinite jest . . . and now, how abhorred in my imagination it is! My gorge rises at it. Here hung those lips that I have kissed I know not how oft. Where be your gibes now? Your gambols? Your songs? Your flashes of merriment, that were wont to set the table on a roar?" At nineteen, when my gorge had risen at the Richters, I'd dashed to the highest peak I could find and effectively summit. After failing to find what I was looking for, I'd come to rest on the lip of an abyss. Across one of his more famous skulls, Richter had run a small squeegee full of blue paint, which smeared haphazardly over the face of humankind. He explained the impetus for his strange technique: "With a brush, you have control. The paint goes on the brush and you make the mark. From experience you know exactly what will happen. With the squeegee you lose control. Not all control, but some control." Just a bit of dynamite in the face of Yorick.

THE DYNAMITE HAD BEEN CAREFULLY removed from the Nietzsche-Haus in my absence. After seventeen years, the interior was clean, new, and sterile. Nietzsche might have found it revolting. It was no longer a house where an occasional troubled visitor could rest his or her head before trekking out into an unforgiving nature: it was now a proper museum and writers' retreat. The anxiety and freedom of the place was all but gone. On my second—and, I fear, final—visit, I arrived on a late-summer morning. It was raining, and I was actually hoping for a little melancholia to ground what seemed like days of gracious hospitality at the Waldhaus. I could not have been more disappointed.

The structure was bursting at the seams with people and light. Laughter from the kitchen wafted up the stairs of the house and greeted me at the front door upon my arrival. I quickly counted five, six, seven voices—and immediately wanted to leave. Instead, I trundled upstairs to my old room and investigated the hallway I'd spent so many long nights traversing. The Richters were gone. The only trace of the artist in the entire house was a piece of stained glass on the second floor, a geometric color grid adorning the west-facing window, and it looked nothing like the skulls I remembered from my youth. On this dreary afternoon the window looked drab and hideously out of place. This was not some Roman Catholic cathedral, I thought in hasty impatience; this was the site where a man—not a saint—tried his best to make peace with the tragedies of life. Where were my smudges and dynamite? Richter's glass was a riff on *4096 Colors*, which he had designed in the 1970s, an eight-foot-square canvas gridded into 4,096 color squares across the spectrum. He'd hired apprentices to paint the piece. I understood that he had some high-minded aesthetic theory in view, but in the narrow confines of the Nietzsche-Haus on a shadowy afternoon it seemed ridiculous, and I had to stifle an urge to break the awful thing then and there. Instead, I managed to concentrate on the walls of the museum.

The house had been converted into a gallery: track lighting illuminated historical sketches of the figures who had visited Sils-Maria to catch sight of the *Übermensch*. More laughter from downstairs. It wasn't just a gallery; it had also become a

hotel of sorts. I could hear that they were talking about Nietzsche and the eternal return—over pastries and cappuccinos. In
1962 Georg Lukács, the Hungarian Marxist, wrote a polemic
against Adorno and the other scholars who had thronged to
Sils-Maria and taken up residence at the Waldhaus. He called
it "the Abysmal Hotel": a grand hotel on the edge of an abyss,
a place of luxury where one could contemplate the existential vacuum, a comfortable gallery from which to view the
end of the world. More laughter: I shuddered to think that
the Nietzsche-Haus itself had become this abysmal hotel,
but it probably had.

I coursed my way down the hallway, taking in the displays:
here was Adorno and his friend Herbert Marcuse, the author
of *One-Dimensional Man*, a book that explained modernity's tendency to stifle self-actualization. And next to them Rilke, Lou
Salomé's lover, who would come to the Engadine regularly.
And there, hanging in the corner of the gallery, was Thomas
Mann, who wrote *Doctor Faustus* with Adorno's help in the
mid-1940s. Mann—profoundly wealthy—had made the Waldhaus, not the Nietzsche-Haus, his second home after World
War II. All these men had attempted to capture something of
Nietzsche.

Mann's *Doctor Faustus* is the story of a man, Adrian
Leverkühn, who takes after Nietzsche in many respects. Bur-
dened with great intellect, Leverkühn, like the original Faust
of Goethe and German lore, is deeply dissatisfied with his
knowledge. It is, after all, just human knowledge. He wants
more. So he intentionally contracts syphilis (what many still
regard as the disease that tipped Nietzsche into insanity) to
heighten his genius by way of madness. Of course he and the
plot quickly degenerate. At the end of the book, obsessed with

the Last Judgment and the Passion of the Christ, Leverkühn calls out to his friends (let's just call them what they are: disciples) to keep him company and witness his self-imposed Crucifixion.

Mann's Faustus attempted to resurrect Nietzsche, but I couldn't help thinking it missed the mark in an important respect. It was written in exile, in light of a Great War—that much sounds Nietzschean—but it was written in Los Angeles. Mann loved it there and would walk his poodle around mansions in Pacific Palisades quite happily. The Nobel Prize winner was dapper and sociable and loved the constant climate. He had escaped great atrocity, so he deserved a bit of good weather, but the opulence of California, the place where decadence came to roost, seemed out of sync with Nietzsche's intellectual project. It seemed like acquiescing to instead of fighting civilization's downward spiral.

I walked past two photographs of Hermann Hesse peering out severely behind black frames. He looked, as always, thoroughly skeptical about something. Perhaps his suspicion was justified. Maybe the dissonance between mundane reality and infinite possibility, between one's social life and stark authenticity, was a source of profound concern, or worse. I turned away from Hesse toward Nietzsche's onetime room.

Lunch had passed again without my noticing. I wasn't hungry. It was now midafternoon, and sunlight began to pour in Technicolor through Richter's window. Nietzsche's bedroom was locked. Certain things were now off-limits. The curator of the museum must have secured the room before he left. Even when it was unlocked, Nietzsche's room was cordoned off during the day: a heavy white rope hung from one side of the olive doorframe. The loose end was tied in a noose and draped over the doorknob. I considered the image for a long time, but then decided to make my own room look presentable before Carol arrived. A family friend was taking Becca for the night, and after Carol heard that the Haus had become uncreepy, she'd agreed to visit that evening. But first we were going to hike the Val Fedoz as a family. One could, according to Nietzsche, be a decadent, but also its opposite in order to find the right treatment for a wretched state.

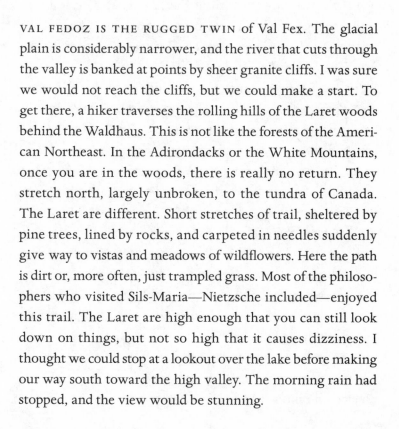

VAL FEDOZ IS THE RUGGED TWIN of Val Fex. The glacial plain is considerably narrower, and the river that cuts through the valley is banked at points by sheer granite cliffs. I was sure we would not reach the cliffs, but we could make a start. To get there, a hiker traverses the rolling hills of the Laret woods behind the Waldhaus. This is not like the forests of the American Northeast. In the Adirondacks or the White Mountains, once you are in the woods, there is really no return. They stretch north, largely unbroken, to the tundra of Canada. The Laret are different. Short stretches of trail, sheltered by pine trees, lined by rocks, and carpeted in needles suddenly give way to vistas and meadows of wildflowers. Here the path is dirt or, more often, just trampled grass. Most of the philosophers who visited Sils-Maria—Nietzsche included—enjoyed this trail. The Laret are high enough that you can still look down on things, but not so high that it causes dizziness. I thought we could stop at a lookout over the lake before making our way south toward the high valley. The morning rain had stopped, and the view would be stunning.

Becca had other ideas. There were flowers in the woods, and she had to gather all of them. Not the large, obvious ones, but the small, easy to drop, easy to lose variety—those were the ones she was after. Why on earth would you want to hike on the trail when the flowers were in the meadows? Because, at first, I wanted to get somewhere. Carol did too, so we both coaxed and coddled Becca along for more than an hour. She would go sprinting, dancing, twirling across the grass, but on the trail, without fail, she became mysteriously tired. It was like walking a poky dog, but then, in a moment of insight, we just gave up. This was adventure enough. We'd reached an open field half a mile from the lookout, and Becca made a dash across the grass toward a ready-made bouquet of buttercups and collapsed in a joyous heap. She'd made it about a mile. She was done for the day.

It was a perfect place to spend an afternoon. A single white chalet perched on a hill a hundred yards from Becca served as a welcome reminder that nature could accommodate human life. And not just any sort of life: Becca at this point was racing again across the high grass, hands outstretched to show us her budding collection. When she reached us, we each got a handful of petals to keep safe, with the quiet request, "Make sure you don't lose them, please." She was polite, but unmistakably insistent. Carol and I settled on a nearby rise and watched our child play. "In every real man a child is hidden that wants to play," Nietzsche said. He is probably right about this, but women philosophers have typically been better about actually playing with the kids.

I considered the petals in my hand. Historically, thinkers have overlooked such things, but Ella Lyman Cabot, a nineteenth-century American philosopher, once wrote of a moment not unlike the one Carol and I were having with Becca and her flowers. Cabot had taken a group of children (she used her family fortune to foster dozens) to pick cherries, and one of the little ones had handed her three of them, not to eat but just to *see*. At first Cabot didn't even know what she was looking at, but then it struck her: "And again, I knew that we were dull, stupid, and blasphemous not to see the overwhelming joy of three cherries all in a row between our fingers." I plucked a ziplock bag from our daypack and carefully stowed Becca's petals. There were flowers aplenty in our New England backyard, but Becca wasn't particularly interested in them. The buds in the Alps were somehow special: something discovered in a world beyond everyday life. Her orientation to things and time had changed slightly on our walk, and it was enough to discern a difference. To Becca, a flower in the Alps was the first of its kind, worthy of attention and protection.

Carol took my hand and pointed to the chalet on the hill. I looked up long enough to see a naked bronze-skinned boy, about seven, duck into the house. A moment later he emerged carrying a pail, which he filled at an outdoor spigot. A little taller than Becca, he was equally tanned from head to toe. His mother, a beautiful heavyset woman in her thirties, joined him outside, placing her brown, bare body on a sun chair. She glanced across the meadow, waved at us lazily, and closed her eyes. There was a complete lack of self-consciousness about her wave. She wasn't an exhibitionist, but she didn't care if people saw her. I'm vaguely uncomfortable with myself at all times, so this was nearly incomprehensible to me. Becca looked up, acknowledged them, and went back to her flowers, and I breathed a sigh of relief that she had yet to inherit my anxieties. In a moment she rose from the ground and took off toward the narrow—shallow—stream that gurgled down the hill, and I managed to stifle the scream of warning that would stop the child in her tracks. She carried on, splashing her way through the summer afternoon.

Fatherhood has traditionally been about limiting a child's sense of possibility. The expression "father knows best" has a correlate: "child does not." Obviously there is something right about this position: a toddler climbing to unsafe heights should be stopped. Children occasionally explore possibilities that are harmful—physically and psychologically—and as parents, it is our place to keep tabs on the threat that existential freedom poses to our kids. But existentialists, following Nietzsche, suggest that our overblown risk aversion doesn't track the actual danger of a particular situation but rather our own sense of anxiety.

Anxiety and dread—in everyday life, they are assiduously avoided. More specifically, we avoid the objects (spiders, exams, shots, clowns, fast-moving rivers) that spur us to anxiety and dread. These experiences, however, have very particular meanings for European philosophers of the nineteenth and twentieth centuries, and these thinkers generally agree that they are not the sorts of things that can or should be avoided. According to existentialists such as Nietzsche, dread has no particular object or cause but rather emanates uncomfortably from the very pit of being human. It is, in Kierkegaard's words, the "sense of freedom's possibility." Imagine all the possibilities you have in life, multiply them by a power of ten and then another power of ten, and finally let yourself consider the many options you have, from a very young age, forbidden yourself. Now, whatever you are feeling—that is something like a weak, attenuated sense of freedom's infinite possibility. The routine of adulthood usually numbs us to this sort of dread, but children do their best to remind us of its force.

Why do we put limits on our children? Of course, virtually all fathers think they are operating in their child's best interests, but I am slowly realizing that most of us protect our children, at least in part, because we are either avoiding or coming to grips with our own anxiety. The more we argue that it is about the child's safety, the more obvious it is that it is all about us. Children remind us, in delightful and painful ways, what it is to be a person. Becca's untethered curiosity, naïve bravery, and complete lack of shame reminded me that I too, at one distant point, possessed these possibilities—and that I had no small amount of trouble doing away with them.

The sky had cleared in the late afternoon. The sun was still high, but it was already beginning to tuck itself behind the mountains to our west. It cast its last warm light across the meadow where our family sat. Carol had packed fruit and a bottle of Barolo: the three of us ate, and the two of us drank. We were about to pack up when it happened: just a few drops at first, then a light mist, then an all-out downpour. The sky was still completely cloudless—just a shimmering, brilliant azure. But it was raining. A lot. It came, literally, out of nowhere. I'd seen sun showers before; on a solo drive across the country in my early twenties, in eastern Montana at twilight, I'd watched a storm gather and release several miles away, under the light of a fading sun. The rain blew horizontally in the upper atmosphere and fell into sunlight. But on the plains, the clouds were still in view. The rain out west made some sense. The rain in Fedoz was something else. The clouds where the rain originated were hidden by mountains, which meant that the droplets seemed to materialize from sun and blue sky. Becca giggled, and we stowed our things quickly. With Becca on my shoulders, we hightailed it back to the Waldhaus.

I knew that sun showers had some mythological significance, but I couldn't bring myself to think about it at the moment. I could only conjure up the other word for such a storm: *serein*, from the French, meaning "serene," or from the Old French *serain*, meaning "evening." It had been a calming rain, at the brink of night, that led into a truly serene experience. We returned to the hotel, peeled off our sopping clothes, and—all three of us—fit ourselves into the oversize claw-footed tub in the Bellavista. We ate a quick dinner, the babysitter arrived, and Carol and I walked hand in hand to the Nietzsche-Haus.

The other guests were still awake, gathered in the downstairs kitchen, chatting happily about Nietzsche's final days. Carol and I climbed the steps to the second floor, and she remarked how cheery the place seemed. I had to agree. We piled into bed and, after several hours, decided to go to sleep. Carol drifted off immediately, and I was left to make myself comfortable in the "abysmal hotel." I was now of two very different minds about it. It was serene, calm, altogether pleasant. The house had become something I could never have imagined on my first trip—an accommodation for lovers and friends. The existential downpour could come, but there was still, somehow, the possibility of a bit of sunshine. All of this is true, but there was something else about the day and place, something uncanny or unnerving about it.

I turned over onto my stomach and propped myself up on my elbows, my abdomen stretched taut across the mattress. I've spent many hours of my life in this position. After meals, whenever I can, I still find a floor and prostrate myself until the uncomfortable fullness, what most people call satisfaction, has faded. My arms and elbows no longer get tired. I stared at Carol for many minutes, brushed the hair out of her face, and resumed my position. She calls it "the Sphinx" and gently reminds me to loosen up on life. Not tonight. I flipped onto my side and drove my thumb, almost unconsciously, into my ribs. This too is a familiar action, a compulsive tick from my youth that somehow reassures me that I am still here, or that the appropriate amount of myself is not.

I hadn't wanted to consider it before, but it was impossible to avoid in the darkness of the room. Sun showers are called something other than "serein." Around the world, this meteorological event has a stunningly similar folkloric meaning. In France they call such a storm "a wolf's wedding"—supposedly the rain is symbolic of the bride's tears. In the Philippines it's even worse: sun showers mark the marriage of the Tikbalang, a mythological trickster who leads travelers astray on their journeys—so badly that they never arrive at their destination. Who would love, much less marry this awful creature is beyond me: he looks like a stretched-out human, gangly and emaciated—except he has a horse's head.

PART III

THE HORSE

To those human beings who are of any concern to me I wish
suffering, desolation, sickness, ill-treatment, indignities—I
wish that they should not remain unfamiliar with profound
self-contempt, the torture of self-mistrust, the wretchedness
of the vanquished: I have no pity for them, because I wish
them the only thing that can prove today whether one
is worth anything or not—that one endures.

—Friedrich Nietzsche,
The Will to Power, 1888

Nietzsche left his summer retreat in Sils-Maria for the last time on September 20, 1888. He was on his way to Turin. His mood and productivity swelled. His vibrancy—I refuse to call it mania—in the Italian city was punctuated ever more frequently by a strangeness that drew the attention of his neighbors and friends. Had he been by himself in Sils-Maria, I have no doubt that these psychological sun showers would have gone undetected for months, even years.

But in Turin, for better and for worse, he had companions who had some trouble understanding the shifts in personality he would undergo during this time.

In 1888 he had begun to sign his letters "Dionysus," and in the following year he took on the moniker of "the Crucified." Days after the new year of 1889 he explained in a letter to his friend Jacob Burkhardt, "basically I am every name in history." His most unusual moments came after long stretches of work, running late into the night as he wrote autobiographical tracts that addressed Dionysian creativity, the deficiencies of Christianity, and the inescapable wake of history. At the same time, he was wrestling with his own past—most explicitly with the enduring ghost of his estranged surrogate father, Richard Wagner. In fact, during his stay in Turin he sat at the piano playing Wagner incessantly from memory. Much to the dismay of his landlord, his finger work would devolve into banging on the keys, mostly with his elbows. Much of this could have been excused had it not been for Nietzsche's fateful, unduly famous episode with the horse.

AS WE BEGAN TO APPROACH the end of our trip, I tried very hard not to think about the end of Nietzsche's life.

It was a lovely day in the Engadine. Becca had seen the horses at the bottom of the hill, below the Waldhaus, earlier in the week, and now she wanted to pet them. I couldn't blame her. At eighteen gorgeous hands, the animals were stately, otherworldly creatures. She wasn't scared at all and, clambering up my back onto my shoulders, pleaded for me to "Get clo-ssss-er,

Papa." I moved in cautiously and let her little hand take hold of the dark mane. The beast didn't move, save for the hoof, which nearly crushed my foot.

Becca is a lovely child—to me, the loveliest: affectionate, even-tempered, curious, playful, so like her mother. She extended her right palm and ran it up toward the animal's ear and slid her left hand under its neck. Just this was a thing of beauty worthy of tears, but I didn't cry. Becca asked to ride the beast, and after a few minutes I managed to convince her that riding in the cart behind the horse would be almost as good. We would take a ride to the Val Fex in the afternoon. After our non-trip to Fedoz, Carol and I agreed that Becca was still too little to make the hike, and cars aren't allowed in the valley. We would go by horse and wagon. Nietzsche would probably not approve, but it was the only way to get there as a family.

The high trail to the glaciers is a narrow path made for one or, at most, two hikers at very close quarters. Switchbacks to traverse, waterfalls to jump, loose stones to negotiate—the trail is more than a little treacherous in dim light. By contrast, the road to Val Fex is wide and rolling. One could walk it with their eyes closed, and the horses probably did. Becca sat in the front of the wagon with the driver, who swung a long whip lazily above the two animals. Carol and I had the back seat to ourselves—to enjoy the view and marvel at how quickly a child can grow up.

This was where Adorno had walked. He'd begun to visit the Waldhaus only after World War II, and he was in his midsixties when he wrote "Aus Sils-Maria," an essay on Nietzsche and his village, which first appeared as notes in a popular German newspaper in October 1966. Adorno's reflections capture a visit to Sils with fellow philosopher Herbert

Marcuse. Both of the men, edging seventy, were on a Nietzschean pilgrimage of sorts. They'd walked to Val Fex, hoping to find something in the footsteps of Nietzsche. But I couldn't imagine that they took the high trail. Their trip was a pale copy of Nietzsche's. And ours paler still. In a certain sense, this was inevitable. Indeed, Nietzsche's days in Turin, playing Wagner by heart, might have delivered him to a similar conclusion. Adorno explains that "a human being only becomes a human at all by imitating other human beings." This might be descriptively true, but the truth was, at least in this case, painful and frustrating. "Today self-consciousness," he writes, "no longer means anything but reflection on the ego as embarrassment, as realization of impotence: knowing that one is nothing."

I looked up at Becca and the man with the whip. At first it didn't look as if he was using it at all, but after a minute or two I noticed that he occasionally, especially on the hills, lowered it enough so that the threads on the end brushed the undulating brown backs. The beasts immediately quickened their pace, and I cringed, waiting for Becca to realize that this form of obedience was hinged to violence. Thankfully, she didn't. For a moment I thought about the surreal picture of Rée, Nietzsche, and Salomé in Lucerne: a woman with a whip and two men in harnesses. The whip whispered across the horses as we rolled slowly up the next incline. How could an animal feel that? What sort of training had to be endured to cultivate this sort of sensitivity?

We began to reach proper altitude, and the valley stretched behind us. High above us was the trail I'd taken early that week, now just a tan thread against a green backdrop. I knew it would soon disappear altogether. From there, one could have seen the hamlet of Fex far below. Adorno had written about the villages that were scattered across the valley floor: they were best viewed from above. Indeed, high above. "From these heights, the villages look as though they had been deposited . from above by light fingers, as if they were movable and without firm foundations. This makes them look like toys that promise happiness to those with giant imaginations: it is as if one could do with them as one pleases." Great heights can make one feel this way. Nietzsche called this the "pathos of distance," and there is probably something to it—the glorious feeling of looking down—but these vistas are merely temporary. The sense of infinite possibility closes so quickly. And the higher one goes in order to get a better, wider, more comprehensive view, the more likely one is to contract altitude sickness. One might also have great trouble reacclimating to lower elevations.

When they weren't wandering around Val Fex, Adorno and Marcuse interviewed the few inhabitants of Sils-Maria who still remembered Nietzsche, the person. An elderly shopkeeper named Zaun had been a boy when the philosopher took refuge in town. He remembered that Nietzsche carried a red parasol in all weather to shield his sensitive head from the elements. Zaun, along with the other boys of the village, would sneak pebbles into the umbrella so they would rain on Nietzsche when he opened it. He was a man whose most genuine attempts to protect himself backfired with stunning regularity. According to Zaun, Nietzsche would chase after them but never catch or harm them. These, I can only assume, were moments of resignation, of accepting his destiny as a man beaten, gently, from all sides.

Our wagon slowed, and Becca let out a peal of laughter.

Luki, a twenty-year-old stallion and one of the largest I'd ever seen, stutter-stepped and defecated. The result was huge and, according to our daughter, hilarious. It fell into a waxed bur-lap bag rigged up to the back of his harness. Obviously there was some rule about the cleanliness of the road to Fex. Luki wasn't finished, and he paused for another moment. Most horses can do it in full stride, but Luki didn't want to. It was a moment too long. The whip gently fell on his back. And then again, not quite so gently. Like it or not, Luki was finished. A beast that is forced to carry his own shit day after day while being whipped—I cannot think of a more appropriate object of compassion. In *Crime and Punishment*, Raskolnikov dreams of witnessing a horse being beaten to death. His response is natural and automatic: to embrace and kiss the poor creature while shielding it from its drunken assailant.

RASKOLNIKOV'S DREAM became Nietzsche's reality. He hugged a horse in Turin's Piazza Carlo Alberto on the morning of January 3, 1889. He then supposedly crumpled to the ground, unconscious. Nietzsche intended to protect the animal from being beaten by its driver, but in the process he succumbed to the pressures—physiological, mental, philosophical—that had confronted him for years. The baroque facade of the Palazzo Carignano, a sign of the Enlightenment and decadence, loomed above him in the plaza, and he fell apart. This was the point where Nietzsche supposedly broke, and most scholars sug-gest that he was never able to pull himself together again in the remaining eleven years of his life. Many books that discuss his philosophy terminate in his fateful meeting with the horse in Turin. There is, however, something false or weak about these accounts: they look away at precisely the point where Nietzsche would encourage greater vigilance. His late study of decadence taught him to be patient in investigating decline and self-destruction. It often takes longer than one thinks, and one is to remain especially clear-eyed as something fully vanishes.

The last decade of Nietzsche's life reveals many things: that life itself outstrips philosophy, that one can really live on in dreams and fantasies, that life and story are inseparable, that degeneration is often regarded as an embarrassment worthy of covering up, that dying at the right time is the greatest challenge of life, that the line between madness and profundity is a faint thread high in the mountains that eventually disappears.

BEHOLD, THE MAN

The highest man . . . would be the man who represented the
antithetical character of existence most strongly . . .

—Friedrich Nietzsche,
The Will to Power, 1888

WE HAD THREE DAYS LEFT IN THE MOUNTAINS, and I had two short books left in my suitcase, *Ecce Homo* and *The Antichrist*, both published years after Nietzsche's mental collapse in Turin. I knew where I wanted to read *Ecce Homo*: off the beaten path, *above* the high trail to Fex, on the lip of an escarpment overlooking the valley. I packed very light—just a water bottle, a headlamp, and my book—and took off before sunrise.

"I'll be back after lunch," I whispered in Carol's ear before leaving.

Nietzsche's last decade was spent yearning for this trail, but he was kept mostly inside, under lock and key and the watchful eye of his mother and sister. Nietzsche's mother had, from the start, tried to compensate for the absence of his father, which produced what I'd always regarded as an unintended but foreseeable consequence: an absolute devotion bordering on absolute codependence. Her son had distanced himself at various times—such as when she meddled with his relationships with women—but as Nietzsche's mental health supposedly declined in 1888, Franziska finally got to care for her elderly child exactly as she pleased. She would be the one taking him for walks now, and she made sure to time them so he wouldn't be able to shout or bellow at her neighbors. She also kept him from walking a fatal path that he often hoped to travel, one charted by a number of thinkers who had inspired Nietzsche in his youth and to whom he returned at the end of his life. One was the Romantic-modernist poet Friedrich Hölderlin.

Hölderlin had confronted the decline of Western civilization nearly a century before Nietzsche. Writing in the aftermath of the French Revolution, in a style that attempted to wed German and ancient Greek thought, he tried to understand the relationship between destruction and creation, and he held, much like Nietzsche, that destruction created the space and opportunity for new birth. In a fragmentary essay titled "Becoming in Dissolution," Hölderlin writes, "in the state between being and non-being, however, the possible becomes real everywhere and . . . in art this is a frightful yet divine dream."

Following the pre-Socratic philosopher Heraclitus, Hölderlin was a "weeping philosopher," one who suffered deeply from what was, at the time, termed "hypochondria" but would today be called depression or anxiety disorder. His psychological fragility made working for a living very difficult, and he was supported largely by his mother. His last years of freedom were spent playing the piano "morning until night." Eventually those free years came to an end, and in 1800 he was institutionalized at the Autenrieth asylum, where he was straitjacketed and forced to wear the Autenrieth mask. Made of leather and wood, the mask was a muzzle that kept a patient from talking or screaming. Hölderlin was force-fed—a hell I've often imagined. And he descended ever more quickly into what most people call madness.

Nietzsche adored Hölderlin's writings and must have felt no small amount of sympathy for a man who imploded in the frenzy of creation. His deep respect for Hölderlin, however, can be traced to a mutual admiration that both thinkers held for an ancient philosopher who came closest to their worldview. It wasn't Heraclitus, but rather Empedocles. Empedocles believed that the world operated under exactly two principles of order: love and strife. His cosmology envisions a dynamic cycle that, in turn, pulls things apart in strife and draws them together in affection, eternally. This is the heart and soul of all creation, according to Empedocles. Both Hölderlin and Nietzsche could wholly accept this description of reality.

ANYWHERE IN THE ALPS can be dangerous. You can make them more or less so by the way you negotiate the terrain.

I took the high trail to Fex, which traversed the mountain range at approximately 7,000 feet, but two hours into the hike, I paused and peered at the top of the range above me that led directly to Piz Tremoggia, at 11,200 feet. I didn't particularly care if I made it there, but I did want to be on the top of something. So I took the approach I'd taken so often as a teenager and went perpendicular to the path. I wouldn't go that far. Just a few thousand feet. I'd done it in my youth, and I was sure it would work again.

Scrambling exists in the amorphous no-man's-land between walking and technical climbing. You do it on all fours like a beast, pulling with your arms and pushing with your legs in tandem. In the Alps, you can take the well-established trails, marked by the Swiss Alpine Club (a group of octogenarians who put all other athletes to shame), or you can create your own path by scrambling. In truth, I've seen very few hikers do this—actually no one—but I'm sure that most scramblers go in the early morning and, like me, take the first hundred feet of the ascent at top speed. They are out of earshot in a matter of minutes and then quickly out of sight. I'm not sure why I bolt off the trail like this: probably because of the fear that I am going to be caught or punished for transgressing some unmarked boundary. Or maybe it is simply the fact that I can. At any rate, on this morning, I tried to move fast.

There are two rules to Alpine scrambling (probably more than two, but I haven't learned them yet). The first one is to "find a line"—that is, find a route you can take without dying. One could use a detailed topographical map, but I have always regarded that as cheating. Scramblers should look for paths with minimal loose rock and avoid any vertical ascents of more than ten feet. Beware of slippery surfaces—slime- or ice-covered rocks—and use good judgment about placing one's boots or, in my case, old sneakers. The second trick to scrambling is not to be deceived by the innocuousness of the term. It might seem that it should be considerably less dangerous than technical climbing, and it would be, if a person were actually roped in on a scramble. If one falls on a technical climb, a belay will (hopefully) catch the person. But scrambling is done with no strings attached. One should be prepared to stay on rock without any assistance and therefore be especially careful of what hikers term "exposure," or the possibility of tipping into thin air.

The climb was easy at first: the mossy grasses of mid-elevation gave me something to clutch, and the grade wasn't particularly steep. Had I slipped, I would've skinned my knees, but that's it. I went up hand over hand, arriving at the first substantial rise without trouble. This one, of course, just let me see more clearly what I was going to climb next. The grass disappeared and was replaced with granite. Two more rises and I'd lost track of my point of departure. I looked in vain, but I figured it probably wasn't my fault: to lose sight of one's recent history is just a function of amateur climbing. I knew I'd started somewhere far below, but God only knew where. I had some idea about my destination, but only vaguely: high above me, somewhere, I would stop. That end point was, it turned out, revealed only over the next several hours. I found a line that ran up the crest of a nameless ridge over Val Fex. And after a time, in the late afternoon, I settled onto a rock ledge, the escarpment that looked roughly like the one for which I had been searching.

This was high enough. Plucking *Ecce Homo* out of my largely empty pack, I promised myself that I'd read only a few pages and then scramble down before darkness fell. Just a couple of pages: "Those who can breathe the air of my writings know that it is an air of the heights, a strong air. One must be made for it. Otherwise there is no small danger that one might catch cold in it. The ice is near, the solitude tremendous—but how calmly all things lie in the light. How freely one breathes! How much one feels beneath oneself." *Ecce Homo*, translated "Behold the Man," is Nietzsche's autobiography. It is the account he gives at the brink of mental collapse. Perhaps it is the story that *allows* him to go over the edge. It is, indeed, the most personal and authentically inauthentic story I've ever read. It is full of bombast and self-aggrandizement, switchbacks and dead ends, what some readers regard as the sign of a deranged mind. "Why I Am So Wise," "Why I Am So Clever," "Why I Write Such Good Books": these are the principal chapter headings of *Ecce Homo*. I agree: Nietzsche would be completely insane were he not aware of his exaggeration. But this is a false bombast that knows itself.

Irony allows one to say two things at once, indeed to express two mutually exclusive realities in a single utterance. It allows one to give voice to love and strife, to indebtedness and ingratitude, to salvation and guilt, triumph and utter defeat all in one breath. "I am the world's best philosopher," "I am the perfect parent," "I have absolute self-knowledge": these impossible instances of hyperbole actually indicate, very honestly, how far they are from the truth. Irony is the language of the two-faced. It allows one to be a decadent and its opposite. Nietzsche admits, "A dual series of experiences, this access to apparently separate worlds, is repeated in my nature in every respect: I am a *Doppelgänger*, I have a second face in addition to the first. And perhaps also a third."

Perhaps these are the ravings of a lunatic or, more specifically, as Julian Young argues, the signs of bipolar disorder. Or
perhaps Nietzsche is directing a reader's attention to the bifurcated nature that underpins much of human reality, the splits
and fractures one experiences in the course of adult life. To
feel deeply the wisdom-tinged sadness of growing older, to understand that one's youth isn't long gone, but rather somewhere forever hidden from view, to face self-destruction
while longing for creation—this is to grapple with *Ecce Homo*.
Being a parent is to live out such a disjunction between duty
and personal freedom—to love a child with one's entire being, but to preserve something of one's identity that parenting
cannot touch. Nietzsche explains how this divided self is not
only possible but inevitable.

Nietzsche picked his title carefully. *"Ecce homo"*: these are
the words of Pontius Pilate when he presents Jesus to the people
before the Crucifixion. By this point Jesus had been badly
beaten, crowned with thorns, and clothed, as a final insult, in
a royal robe. Behold the man, mocked in all his frailty and suffering. Behold the man, who would feign to be the Messiah.
In Caravaggio's 1605 rendering of the scene, Pilate, dressed as
a sixteenth-century nobleman-scholar, stands in front of Jesus
and looks directly at the viewer. It is as if Pilate has just raised
the curtain on a would-be Messiah. His gesture and sweeping
hand speak clearly: "Look, I told you so. He's just a man." And
then there's the man, who is arguably beside the point—just
an average-size guy with shaggy hair and a crown of thorns,
looking down, ashamed of the fix he's in. Behind the man is
his tormenter, a strange two-faced figure who covers the condemned in a robe out of hatred and pity. Of course, Jesus is
supposed to be the quintessential divided being—completely

man and completely God—but in *Ecce Homo* he is human-all-too-human. At the end of *Ecce Homo* all that remains is the mystery of an empty tomb.

It began to rain gently. It was late afternoon. I didn't want to, but I would have to leave soon. I looked over the edge of the cliff and saw that things dropped off precipitously for about two hundred feet and then leveled off a bit. *Ecce Homo* was about "exposure," drawing oneself out into the open and revealing the parts that are typically off-limits. Rock climbers talk about "exposure" with a distinct mix of admiration and horror, and they should. There is a sort of deadly triumph in confronting it. Quoting Ovid, Nietzsche writes, "*Nitimur in vetitum.*" "Strive for the forbidden." In his last days in Turin, as Nietzsche completed *Ecce Homo*, the Swedish playwright August Strindberg wrote to him: "I will, I will be mad."

Why were Nietzsche and Hölderlin so drawn to Empedocles? It wasn't just for his cosmology of love and strife. According to myth, Empedocles was a mountain climber of sorts. One day, he climbed Mount Etna, the massive active volcano on the east end of the island of Sicily, two and a half times as large as the more famous Mount Vesuvius, which buried Pompeii. Empedocles scrambles to the lip of Etna and leaps to his death.

This, however, isn't just any suicide; Empedocles's death, according to legend, is the beginning of an eternal life. When he is incinerated by the flames, he is granted immortality. Dying at the right time, in this reading of the story, has its advantages. As a young man, Nietzsche read Hölderlin's *The Death of Empedocles* and was immediately enraptured. In *Ecce Homo* he returns to its theme explicitly: "One must pay dearly for immortality," he writes, "one has to die several times while

one is still alive." The Roman poet Horace regards Empedocles's death as the quintessential act of creation, the exception
that proves the rule—artists have the tendency, but also the
permission, to destroy themselves for the sake of originality.

I looked up from my damp book and down the mountain.
It struck me that I'd forgotten something about "finding a
line": a scrambler is supposed to chart a trail that one can easily descend. In dry conditions, this would not have been a huge
challenge. But the rocks were now slick, and the light rain
continued to fall. Many stranded climbers are not climbers at
all—they are scramblers who have gotten too far into an ascent and freeze at the prospect of falling. When this happens,
and the Fates are smiling, the helicopters are brought in to
airlift them out of their embarrassment to safety. I'd watched
this happen on my last trip to the Alps: two hikers in red pon-
chos had scrambled to ten thousand feet on Corvatsch and gotten stuck on a ridge they couldn't negotiate. As the chopper
came to their rescue, I was mortified for them. I would take
my chances in the rain, but I'd be careful this time.

As I inched my way to lower elevations and twilight approached with startling speed, I remembered a detail I'd pre-
viously overlooked in Hölderlin's *The Death of Empedocles*. Most
of the poem is set on Mount Etna. The philosopher is on the
mountain, contemplating his destiny, when his loved ones
reach him. His wife entreats him to come down from the ledge,
to make another go at living a normal life. But her begging
convinces him that there is only one way to descend. If one has
to be implored to back away from the edge, maybe the flames
really do have their appeal. Empedocles jumps not to become
immortal but to prove that he has already transcended the
long suffering of life. The fire consumes him until absolutely

nothing is left, or almost nothing. Far from Etna, a single bronze sandal falls from the skies. Empedocles's shoe is all that remains of his fatal or divine experiment.

Perhaps *Ecce Homo* is Nietzsche's version of Empedocles's leap. He doesn't slip; he knows exactly what he is doing. It looks like madness, and perhaps it is, but it is *his* madness.

Or perhaps *Ecce Homo* is simply Nietzsche's sandal.

BY THE TIME I REACHED the Waldhaus, it was after lunch. It was also after dinner, and darkness had consumed the mountains. Carol was understandably seething. The second I walked through the door, she moved from worried sick to utterly enraged.

"Where the *fuck* were you?" She curled her lips back and whispered through bared teeth.

We quieted Becca, who had spent the early evening fretting that Papa had either fallen to his death or abandoned her. Carol led her into the other room, flipped on the television, which had remained silent during our stay, and turned up the volume. This was not good.

Carol's temper had been cool and pleasant at the beginning of the journey, but in recent days, as my trips to the mountains had become longer and more frequent, her patience had waned. Now it was gone. She came back into the room and let me have it as only a Kantian can—quietly, brutally, irrefutably. No, she was not going to accept my feeble attempts to defend myself, accusing me of exactly the sort of immature bullshit I'd been insisting was the wrong way to read my existential tour guide.

I was such an entitled prick. What happened to the equally shared parenting that we'd agreed upon? What did I mean hiking up alone into the hills and leaving her to take care of Becca? If I really wanted to be alone, maybe she would just take Becca and go home. Then I could grow old and insane all by myself.

Of course, she was right. Eventually I apologized (which I really meant), promised not to take any more unannounced treks (which I think I meant), and turned to bathing our little girl and getting her ready for bed. Things were going relatively smoothly until I went to brush her teeth. Becca is usually so tractable and good-natured that I almost expect her to be this way all the time. Typically she just opens her mouth and I scrub her tiny white teeth, but tonight was different—a suitable punishment for a father who'd temporarily gone off the rails.

I saw her masticatory muscles seize up before I even asked her to open her jaws. Then she just shook her head. I asked again, and she opened her mouth long enough to say, "No thanks," chuckling fiendishly behind her clenched lips. I raised my voice, but that just made her bite down harder. This was a joke—I knew—but I wasn't laughing. I'd not told her the story of Nietzsche's lion, the free spirit who says "No" to authority, or Herman Melville's "Bartleby the Scrivener," a short story written in 1853 that considers the Nietzschean possibility that freedom is realized in a self-destructive refusal to submit. But some children are born with these lessons, and she now was using them against me.

Melville's Bartleby is the scribe of a Wall Street lawyer, and he slowly, systematically refuses to take on the tasks that his life demands. He wasn't always so difficult. At one point he was the consummate employee (cheerful, dutiful, obedient), but then he is asked to proofread one too many boring legal memos. And he snaps. For no apparent reason, he responds with an answer that haunts the rest of the story: "I would prefer not to." When he is asked to do his job—he "would prefer not to"; when asked to leave the law office (because obviously he has been fired), he "would prefer not to." Of course we want to know why he would prefer not, but there's no reason. Bartleby doesn't need to give a reason. This is a story about volition. He continues to refuse everything. Even food and water. So he's found four days later, dehydrated and starved. Stone dead.

Becca's life as Bartleby had begun two years before with a "No"—emphatic and unexplained—at my request to please get her shoes. It was, by all accounts, a reasonable request. We were going to the park, the park that she absolutely loved, and parks require footwear. Eventually I'd gotten her shoes on, but the trouble continued. At dinner that night and many nights after, the simple "No" morphed into a very well enunciated, disturbingly calm "No, I won't." No, she would not eat beans or oranges or grapes or yogurt or pasta. No, she would not eat them at the table, on the sofa, in her chair. She would not eat them here or there; she would not eat them anywhere. I'd been at a complete loss, still was, and largely am. Becca helped me understand that this short story is disturbing precisely to the extent that it reflects a deep and unsettling truth about ourselves, one that nineteenth-century authors like Melville and Nietzsche had begun to tap into: beneath the reasonable habits of our lives hides a little inexplicable something that has the ability to opt out, even against our better judgment. And I wanted nothing more than to quash this little something in Becca.

Carol leaned her head into the bathroom and almost smiled. "What goes around comes around, Papa."

I remember thinking that the "terrible twos" are often described as a stage, as a temporary period of parental discomfort that's transcended by the time the little ones get all their teeth. For many optimistic parents this is the birth of autonomy, the point at which individuals start to determine their own lives (instead of letting other forces do the determining for them). And this autonomy is to be fostered so that children eventually become responsible adults, well-functioning members of a well-ordered society. But my day with *Ecce Homo* and my young Nietzschean led me to fear that this is all just wishful thinking.

Freedom allows us to act as responsible agents, but it also allows us to do otherwise. The very thing that we are to cultivate in our children—a free will—is the very thing that can, at least sometimes, make us lose the little person we love so deeply and painfully. The prospect of which is beyond terrifying. Parenting a toddler is difficult for a host of well-known reasons. But ultimately, at least for this parent, its pains have little to do with the way my daughter defies my specific wishes, or even with the prospect of her doing so for the rest of my life. It has everything to do with the fear that comes along with being inextricably bound to a little creature who willfully, gleefully can disregard what is obviously in her own best interest.

Becca was still biting down and laughing, and I knew, remembering Hölderlin's mask and my own father's parenting tactics, that adjusting a body by force could be life-altering. I wouldn't do that. At least not today. She slipped away and skipped off into the bedroom. She'd won: her teeth could rot exactly as she pleased.

How did Empedocles or Nietzsche cultivate the existential

defiance or courage that led each of them up the mountain? It probably started something like this—in a very simple refusal to act on behalf of one's obvious self-interest. There remains a life-affirming glee in such a refusal—a quiet temptation that even the most well-adjusted person feels at various points. It is the freedom to be otherwise, to act against all odds. Turning the bathroom light off, I hoped—I'm sure not for the last time—that my daughter would not become a philosopher.

STEPPENWOLF

*This painting—that which we humans call life and
experience—has gradually become, is indeed still fully
in the process of becoming, and should thus
not be regarded as a fixed object . . .*

—Friedrich Nietzsche,
Human, All Too Human, 1878

IT WAS THE FIRST WAKING MOMENT OF OUR FINAL DAY. I adjusted the blankets of our bed, leaned into Carol one last time, and began my predawn prowl. In the darkness, I rummaged through the suitcase for what I thought was Nietzsche's *The Antichrist*, but only came up with a thin novel written by another recluse of the Waldhaus decades after Nietzsche's death. I remembered that this book was one of the reasons I had wanted to revisit this place. So at 4:00 a.m., two hours before daybreak, as the full moon hung over Maloja, I headed for Nino's room in the turret of the hotel. It was locked, but I settled comfortably in a sofa at the foot of the steps.

In the days of Adorno, Mann, and Marcuse, the Waldhaus was frequented by another now-famous visitor. He stayed at the hotel, in total, for 370 days. His room was the most modest in the building, and as was his wont, he stayed mostly out of the way. He was a gaunt man with a sharp jaw and nose. His spare frame belied an almost superhuman physical strength, cultivated from years of Alpine skiing. When he smiled—at least for photographs—his lips remained pursed, just a straight line, which stood in marked contrast to his eyes, wide and gleaming. Mann was one of his best friends, and Mann envied him: he was, in Mann's words, "so much further ahead of me as regards spiritual freedom." The man was much older than he looked, and he fought the onset of physical decay to the very end. If there is one Waldhaus guest who came closest to Nietzsche's personal disposition, it was this one. This was the Nobel laureate Hermann Hesse, the author of my beat-up copy of *Steppenwolf*.

Born in 1877, Hesse almost immediately became a problem child. He was headstrong and independent from the start. When he was four years old, his mother wrote of her son,

> The little fellow has a life in him, an unbelievable
> strength, a powerful will, and . . . a truly astonishing
> mind. How can he express all that? It truly gnaws at
> my life, this internal fighting against his tyrannical
> temperament, his passionate turbulence . . . God
> must shape this proud spirit, then it will become
> something noble and magnificent—but I shudder

to think what this young and passionate person might become should his upbringing be false or weak.

He was, I guess, the sort of child one could easily love and detest. Indeed, his parents struggled for many years with the decision to either keep him at home or allow professionals to raise the boy. His father reflected that despite the embarrassment, perhaps it would be better to "put him in an institution or farm him out to strangers." Hesse was astute—about everything—so he was aware, from the beginning, of his parents' ambivalence. This awareness quickly grew into fear and anger: the sense that one is always on the edge of parental abandonment.

The headaches and insomnia began before Hesse reached his teenage years and got significantly worse when he was admitted to the prestigious church school at Maulbronn at the age of thirteen. He lasted at the school for less than a year, eventually being placed in the care of a pastor at Bad Boll, in southern Germany. Like Nietzsche, Hesse's first real love was disastrous, and at the age of fifteen, after being rejected by the twenty-two-year-old Eugenie Kolb, he bought a handgun and disappeared. He reappeared a day later. He'd come to the edge of the abyss, but managed to step back. In September of that year (still fifteen, mind you), a frustrated Hesse longs for his revolver: "What I would not give for death! . . . I have lost everything now: home, parents, love, belief, hope, myself . . ." In the next year, he managed to get to Stuttgart, sell off some of the philosophy books that had underpinned his tremendous erudition, and used the money to buy another gun. But it remained, for the time being, unused.

Hesse began to read Nietzsche at the time when many young men do, at the age of seventeen. It was 1895, and Hesse was living in Basel, the town where Nietzsche had begun as a philosopher. By this time Nietzsche's health had declined severely, and he was living on only by the good graces of his sister, Elisabeth, and his mother. In 1893, Elisabeth had returned to Europe after emigrating with her husband, Bernhard Förster, to Paraguay in 1886. Förster was a full-throated anti-Semite and had traveled to South America with the hopes of establishing a "New Germania," based on a pure vision of Teutonic culture. When this utopia didn't come to fruition, Förster killed himself. Four years after that, his wife, Nietzsche's sister, returned to her Swiss home. Elisabeth would have to further their political and ideological agenda in other, more surreptitious ways.

The year 1895 was an important one in Nietzsche's life as an author. He had achieved a degree of fame he'd never experienced in his middle years, and true scholars, like Hesse, were beginning to explore the nuanced implications of his writing. Nietzsche had written most of *The Antichrist* in 1888, before his collapse, but owing to its radical nature, its publication was delayed for seven years. When it finally came out, in 1895, it stood as a précis of Nietzsche's philosophy on the whole. The book's title, often traced to the biblical Antichrist, has less to do with this figure than it does with the "man of lawlessness" who rejects out of hand traditional theology and faith in the Divine. Lawlessness exposes the final erosion of religious authority and signals the end times of modern civilization. According to Scripture, the Antichrist is ultimately destroyed by the second coming of Jesus, but Nietzsche didn't put much stock in this part of the story. *The Antichrist* is Nietzsche's most pointed attack on Christian slave morality, a thinker's last attempt to transcend the defining character of modernity—its weakness, its pity, its thirst for revenge. As night fell on the nineteenth century, a growing number of individuals, including Hesse, resonated with the aspiration of *The Antichrist*.

The last decade of Nietzsche's life, one of almost complete incapacitation, was, ironically, the most pivotal in securing his reputation as a philosopher. Readers such as Hesse began to take his work seriously, but this was also the point at which Nietzsche's sister would initiate her exclusive takeover of his literary estate, the moment at which his writings began to be given over to German propagandists who would eventually fit his "philosophy with a hammer" to the Third Reich. After the death of their mother, Elisabeth moved Nietzsche to Weimar in the hopes of starting a Nietzsche cult, which never materialized. What was constructed in Weimar, however, was the Nietzsche Archive, and it is here, in 1934, where Adolf Hitler was photographed nose-to-nose with a bust of Nietzsche. All this was not Nietzsche's own doing, and certainly not his intent, but it happened all the same. One is never fully in charge of their legacy.

Many of Nietzsche's writings express an enduring worry about the future, the claim that his philosophy would be understood only and always "the day after tomorrow." In *The Antichrist*, Nietzsche writes that some men are born posthumously. He was probably correct, given that he came into view and achieved notoriety only after he'd largely stopped writing. The problem with being understood posthumously, however, is that it is vastly easier to be misunderstood. And Elisabeth did misunderstand—or, more likely, misuse—her brother. That his writings on nonconformity and freedom, shot through with self-reflective irony, could be appropriated by the Nazis remains one of the true tragedies of nineteenth- and twentieth-century philosophy. Thankfully, there were thinkers like Hesse who sought to preserve something of the spirit that had animated Nietzsche's later works.

HESSE WAS NOT NIETZSCHE'S DISCIPLE. In many respects he walked with Nietzsche only to later depart, rejecting the story of master morality Nietzsche had espoused in *Thus Spoke Zarathustra*. The will to power seemed simplistic and futile, especially in light of Nietzsche's admission later in life that the powers of decay and decadence were inescapable, but Hesse still admired the artistry of *Zarathustra*. So instead of fixating on Zarathustra's speeches, the literal content of the sermons, which were filled with vainglory, Hesse focuses on the complexity of the character himself, the way that Zarathustra, and Nietzsche, represented the internal struggles of a multifaceted nature. Is it not possible, Hesse asked, that to possess such enduring tensions is the lot of being human?

This fracturing, for Hesse, is not a sign of madness but rather of simply being alive. He points a reader back to Nietzsche, who, in his own words, was not interested in harboring a single immortal soul but rather a variety of mortal ones. *Ecce Homo* is difficult to grasp, among other reasons, because Nietzsche is and is not so very many things—at once. And it is never clear—either in Hesse or Nietzsche—that these souls can live normally in long-standing agreement. Beginning in 1919 with the novel *Demian*, Hesse's interest in Nietzsche ratcheted up, as did the quality of his work, as he began to address the fate of this divided self.

I'd read *Demian* at the age of thirty as I exited my first marriage. Hesse was married three times, and *Demian* is a coming-of-age story, so I thought it might provide a bit of insight. At the time, I'd already fallen in love with Carol (that happened long before the divorce) and I was beginning to think through what was, for me, a difficult question that could be voiced in two registers: How can one love in the right way while being so quietly dissatisfied with life? or How can one love while being so mired in oneself? Also at the time, I was reading a host of American philosophers—Ralph Waldo Emerson, William James, and Josiah Royce—who were interested in the possibility of transcendence and love. *Demian* had fit in rather nicely.

Hesse's *Demian* is the story of a man, Emil Sinclair, who is in need of salvation from the doldrums and illusions of everyday life. He is desperately looking for something else, something beyond mere appearances. Sinclair finds his spiritual mentor in Max Demian and his mother, Frau Eva. At first Demian appears as merely a very smart childhood friend. When the two are in confirmation class, Demian leans over to inform Sinclair, "You knew all along that your sanctioned world was only half the world and you tried to suppress the second half the way the priests and teachers do. You won't succeed. No one succeeds in this once he has begun to think." Forbidden and buried, this need for something transcendent remains the silent motive of Sinclair's life. Over the course of the book, a reader comes to realize that Demian isn't just a smart friend but rather a hidden aspect of Sinclair himself, a wellspring of spiritual energy that Sinclair can tap at any time if he possesses the proper self-knowledge. At the end of the book, wounded on a battlefield, Sinclair, with Demian's help, discovers that he is capable of saving himself, and a reader is left to assume that he does.

If this sounds pat or simple, it is. But it was perfect when I was entering a new relationship: Demian's self-exploration and the final uniting of the real and the ideal is what remarriage is supposed to be all about. In the ashes of divorce, a fallen, hapless creature somehow manages to achieve something of the ideal.

Demian is a tale of inner strength, of the triumph of self-knowledge, but in reality such victories are temporary or pyrrhic. That is why, a decade later, after Hesse's first failed marriage, he wrote *Steppenwolf*, which has been called Nietzsche's psychological biography. It is also Hesse's novelistic auto-biography. And most obviously, most directly, it is the tale of a man-beast, Harry Haller, and I found it making more and more sense as I approached the sixth year of my second marriage.

STEPPENWOLF HAD RECENTLY BECOME my favorite, but my reading it in the Waldhaus in the early hours of the day was not going particularly well. I was moving very slowly, in the semiconscious state between darkness and daylight, when one reads and rereads the same passage repeatedly. I couldn't seem to get past the opening pages: a bourgeois narrator informed me that he'd discovered a manuscript written by a tenant, a quiet gentleman by the name of Harry Haller.

Haller, however, is only seemingly quiet. Haller believes—he knows—that beneath his good manners and the quiet fa-cade of his everyday life is a beast, a wolf from the high plains, a real "hairy howler." This awful truth was the shadow of his waking life, an abiding, destructive presence that shrank at high noon but grew immense as the day slipped away. The narrator said that he wouldn't bother telling the story if he believed that Haller's disposition was unique and could be chalked up as "the pathological fancies of a single isolated case of a diseased temperament." But Haller wasn't unique. "I see something more in them," the narrator continues. "I see them as a document of the times." It is a sickness that "by no means attacks the weak and worthless only . . ."

I was drifting off again, and I roused myself to get a cup of coffee at the *Halle* so that I could read more attentively. But en route I realized that the sun was now fully up, as was my family, who came to greet me at the entrance to the dining room. We would have a bite of yogurt and cereal, play with Becca on the playground outside the hotel, and then drop her off at an impromptu nursery school with a bunch of German friends she had met during her stay. Then Carol and I would make a last-day hike to Val Fex, perhaps Nietzsche's favorite haunt.

AS WE REACHED THE TRAILHEAD to the valley, I arrived at a conclusion that I'd tried to avoid for weeks: this trip had been a failure. A search for the *Übermensch* had become a family affair—brimming with tender moments, routine tasks, and playdates. The attempt to be free, to retrace a path that I'd taken in my youth, had been cut short by my family obligations, and the journey had slowly morphed into a holiday taken in honor of Nietzsche's memory rather than anything genu-

inely, authentically Nietzschean. I had proven unable or unwilling to stop its gradual decline into mundane life. Harry
Haller had similar thoughts, but he, unlike most of us, gave
them free rein: "A wild longing for strong emotions and sensations seethes in me," he writes, "a rage against this toneless,
flat, normal and sterile life. I have a mad impulse to smash
something, a warehouse perhaps, or a cathedral, or myself, to
commit outrages."

I entered Val Fex with Carol and these mad impulses, walking at a pace I knew was unsustainable, at least for her. How
fast could we go together? That was the question I wanted to
answer. I never found out, or rather I discovered an answer I
wasn't expecting: twenty minutes later, cresting a small hill,
I slipped on a loose rock and wrenched the knee I'd twisted in
my first week in Sils-Maria. Carol slowed down so I could keep
up. I walked gingerly behind her and raged at myself. Haller
was an educated man, but "what he had not learned, however,
was this: to find contentment in himself and his own life. The
cause of this apparently was that at the bottom of his heart he
knew all the time (or thought he knew) that he was in reality
not a man, but a wolf of the Steppes."

There were more hikers than usual on the low trail. It was
as if everyone in the surrounding villages had voted to make a
humiliation of my life. The cottage at the mouth of the glacial
valley was usually closed and silent this early in the day, and
that had been my hope, but a handful of hikers were already
sitting inside eating apple strudel. As we passed the make-
shift restaurant, a German couple nodded at us while we made
our way into the mountains, and I thought I heard something
on the wind that made me shudder: "*Schafe, Schafe, Schafe.*" I
was sure they were making fun of me: "Sheep, sheep, sheep,"

in English. I took Carol's hand and did my best to enjoy my last day.

Some of the most magnificent mountains of the Alps are not, in my opinion, the snowcapped ones. They are foothills—completely green, lightly variegated by waterfalls and trails. But in the Alps, foothills are not gradual inclines but walls of earth that completely obscure the genuine mountains they lead to. Jutting out of the ground, they ascend directly to the heavens. We were walking parallel to one of these monochromatic slabs, and now that I was traveling a bit slower, I had a chance to look. The ridge was a mile off, across the perfectly flat glacial plain. I had to crane my neck to see the top, and the grassy "hill" filled my entire angle of vision. The only clue that the ridge was actually far away were the tan insects that roamed around its base, insects that could have only been cows. Losing all sense of proportion is one of the inevitable consequences of hiking in the mountains for any extended period of time.

Carol paused on the trail and pulled me close. "Thank you for bringing us here," she whispered.

I nestled my face against her curly head and looked over her shoulder across the valley. A cloud passed across the sun, and as the ridge fell into darkness, its top and bottom edge vibrated and gave off an almost audible pitch, the sound of clenching one's teeth. Freedom against the backdrop of nothingness. I'd been playing with the inside of my bottom lip for most of the week, and I finally bit through.

And then I saw them, just a few at first, running single file across the top of the range. Mountain goats—the chamois I'd dreamed of, but never found, in my youth.

In *Beyond Good and Evil*, Nietzsche insists, "Here among this most remote realm of ice and rock—Here one has to be a hunter and chamois-like." Triumphant at last, I pointed them out to Carol. We were, I thought, too far away to see the male's short, curved horns. During mating season they would use these horns to compete, sometimes brutally, for the affection of females. Agonistic impulses are the rule, not the exception in nonhumans. I'd never seen a chamois in person, much less five sprinting in a row. They were wonderful climbers and, from what I could remember, social but independent creatures, preferring to stay in small same-sex groups for most of the year. I told Carol all about them, with the self-assured pride that only a middle-aged male philosopher could muster. The five animals passed high above us. And then another five. And then another.

"Those aren't mountain goats!" Carol blurted. They were sheep: *Schafe, Schafe, Schafe.* Dozens of them. Her laughter echoed through the hills. It was, I could later admit, somewhat humorous: we were hiking with Nietzsche, the archenemy of docility and domestication, yet at the same time we were being overtaken by the flock. The animals were making good time across the high ground. Carol and I kept walking, and we followed our woolly companions toward the glaciers. Moments later, another train of animals passed us, and now I saw that the sheep were everywhere above us on the cliffs—a hundred at least. They'd looked like rocks at first, but they were moving at various speeds, at a distance that made the slower animals appear stationary. All of us were moving in unison, in the same direction.

Carol and I made our way as quickly as we could across the low ground, glancing up occasionally to see that we weren't falling too far behind our new companions. The animals were going somewhere together, as were we. I was sure we would hit the ice at eight thousand feet and all our journeys would be unceremoniously over. But for the time being, we slowly con-verged, and I had time to think about Henry Haller and his half-domesticated nature.

Harry's bifurcated self was, in fact, the bane and delight of his existence for much of *Steppenwolf*. At one point Haller had been a public intellectual, even a reasonably successful one, but more recently he'd lost his job and his family and begun to embrace a solitary, lupine existence. He admits, "I like the contrast between my lonely, loveless, hunted and thoroughly disordered existence and this middle-class family life . . . there is something in it that touches me despite my hatred for all it stands for." Haller was drawn by, and to, this divided reality—pulled to it like a man tied to a horse on the way to the gallows. Middle age greeted Haller as it does many people, as the dawning of regret. "I do not regret the past," Haller explains. "My regret was for the present day, for all the countless hours and days that I lost in mere passivity and that brought me nothing, not even the shocks of awakening."

Haller's dejection was real, but so too was the fact that he'd lived an altogether pleasant, even profoundly privileged exis-tence. It was largely the life of the mind, one of philosophy and high culture. His life "had wandered in a maze of unhappiness that led to renunciation and nothingness; it was bitter with the salt of all human things; yet it had laid up riches, riches to be proud of. It had been for all its wretchedness a princely life." This had always bothered me about Haller: How could a princely life still, after all is said and done, lead one to renun-ciation and bitterness? As I'd come to enjoy adulthood, this worry had only intensified. Privilege and leisure did nothing to mitigate the effects of existential crisis but rather heightened the sense that despite one's best attempts, life was still largely unfulfilling. Most of modern life is geared toward achieving material success, but only after it is attained is its hollowness painfully apparent.

Haller wanders the streets at night and carefully avoids going home—absolutely nothing awaits him there. One evening as he prowls through town, he passes a man carrying a placard that reads:

ANTICHRIST EVENING ENTERTAINMENT

MAGIC THEATRE

ENTRANCE NOT FOR EVERYONE

Nietzsche's *The Antichrist* begins in precisely the same way: "This book belongs to the most rare of men." This is what Haller has been looking for: exclusive entrance to something other than his normal, conscious life—the permission to be lawless. *Steppenwolf* is a story of Haller's slow and halting pilgrimage to the Magic Theatre, to what turns out to be a metaphorical fun house of his mind, filled with doors and mirrors and characters from his almost-forgotten past. What lies beneath the surface of Haller's life? What lurks in the unspoken? It turns out that it isn't just the Steppenwolf, the bestial shadow of a dissatisfied man. It is more insane, but also more hopeful than that.

I slipped again, this time on something greasy and slick, and went down hard on my left side. Carol turned around to find her husband prostrate, smeared in a thick, almost black substance. We were a mile from the glaciers, walking parallel to the runoff, which roiled out of the mountain and crashed down the valley as a crystal-blue torrent. Cows grazed nearby and came to the river for water. The sheep continued to stream up the ridge. It wasn't hundreds but thousands of animals, moving in unison. I picked myself up. Everything tasted of blood and manure. If only we could get a bit higher, away from all these goddamn creatures. I turned uphill, and Carol followed behind me. The dizziness of walking too much and eating too little had begun days before, but I'd ignored it, even relished it. In the last hour it had fully overtaken me. Every step was like sliding on oil. We found a flat, sun-drenched rock several hundred feet above the river, and Carol convinced me to sit down.

The sheep had also slowed their pace. They'd come to a crevasse and were bottlenecking on the ridge approximately a thousand feet above us. Looking down the valley, we could see more animals on their way. At this distance, the growing herd was just a fuzzy patch of static on a green backdrop. The sound of the sheep mixed with the roar of the river. I lay down on the rock with my head in Carol's warm lap. And everything slowly went dark. In "Assorted Opinions and Maxims," Nietzsche writes, "What we sometimes neither know nor feel during our waking hours . . . in dreams we understand absolutely, unequivocally."

THE SUN IS DIRECTLY OVERHEAD. All I feel is the roar of the river and the stone beneath my head. The sheep and Carol are gone. I am unperturbed by their absence. Even relieved. It is, in the end, better this way. I can make real progress without them. These thoughts arise from the depths in an uncontrolled, unphilosophical fashion. I get to my feet in a similar way and, rolling the waistband of my pants back so they cinch around my now-teenage hips, begin to fly toward the glaciers.

The dizziness is gone, and my feet are, for the first time in days, maybe years, truly steady. The afternoon stands still, and I make incredible time. As the sun sets, I crest Piz Platta, the mountain from my youth, dozens of miles away. Without pause, I'm on Corvatsch, and I come to rest on the gravel-strewn and pockmarked ice. The temperature drops, and my head throbs at the root of my tongue. My ear begins to bleed. Not a lot—just enough to drip at a steady rate onto my shoulder and chest. I could bed down, but I know what the night brings.

At last, I return to it: a crevasse splitting Corvatsch that stretches lengthwise across my path. It is just shy of six feet wide, two hundred feet to the bottom. Just the right size. The sun is gone, the twilight is fading, and the void before me fantastically dark. The crack is long enough that it seems to taper at the ends, bending like Hesse's straight-edged grin. It smiles up, breathes softly, and beckons.

I set my pack down at the very edge of the void, remove my shoes and socks, and place them next to my coat on the frozen ground. I strip down to my skin and carefully fold my shirt and pants, tucking them under my pack so they don't blow away. Wiping the blood from my ear one last time, I bend down to check that the ground at the lip of the abyss is firm. I don't want to slip. Empedocles, Nietzsche, Rée, Nino: I want to make sure my sudden descent is not mistaken for an accident.

BECOME
WHO YOU ARE

They both listened silently to the water, which to them
was not just water, but the voice of life, the voice of
Being, the voice of perpetual Becoming.

—Hermann Hesse,
Siddhartha, 1922

WHEN I WOKE UP, THERE WAS BLOOD IN MY MOUTH, and a small sharp stone had driven into my left earlobe. I couldn't feel my arm, and a hot liquid had pooled in my shoes.

After many minutes with me resting in her lap, Carol's legs had fallen asleep and she'd gently placed my sleeping head on the ground beside her. I'd rolled onto my side and buried my left cheek into the granite. She'd shielded most of my body from the sun, but my lower legs and feet were bathed in warm light.

The sheep had reappeared—a gathering storm of white wool on the mountainside. I opened my eyes and looked up at Carol for a long moment. She eventually noticed, stared back, and slid her leg back under my head.

"Here they come, love," she said, pointing across the valley.

The bottleneck of animals had finally broken, and they came pouring down the mountain, one after another, over crevasses and ditches, flying, floating, on ibex legs. They weren't running or exerting themselves. Just letting gravity do its work. Beautiful, if slightly absurd. Their bleating was now fully audible over the sound of the river. I started to count them, but I lost track at 490. There had to be upward of a thousand. Not a single one threw itself over the edge.

Carol joked that it would be somehow appropriate if they trampled us to death—two philosophers stampeded by the herd. The whole idea was so surreal and funny it could only be the truth. Jesus, was it funny. I laughed until I cried. At some point Carol realized that I was actually just crying, more than I ever had. She held me, and let me let it go.

I wiped my eyes. Nothing—not the valley, not the trail, not the river, not the sheep, not loving, not living, not dying—had changed in seventeen years. It never would. Or rather, it would change in exactly the same way. Love and strife remained. I'd been here before, once on Piz Corvatsch, once high in the White Mountains, many times. Everything, every tension and vibration of life remained the same. But my afternoon dream in the Val Fex had done something to me. Some days I can still feel it. It gave me just a hint: life does not change, but the attitude you bring to it might. And this is not a trivial adjustment. In fact, it may be the only meaningful adjustment that is possible. For a moment, I was happy, genuinely happy, happier than I've ever been, that I was still here. Right here, not somewhere else. The awful abyss, the existential terror, the feeling of inadequacy and privation—none of it mattered. It was, at worst, a figment of my imagination. It was as if I had finally come to—or realized that, after a long and frustrating investigation, I was simply asking the wrong sort of question. For just an instant, nothing frightened me and I longed for neither height nor depth. Then the moment passed, the doubt returned, and *Steppenwolf* remained.

As *Steppenwolf* became more popular, Hesse remarked that it was the most misunderstood of all his books. It isn't, as many readers assume, about the self at war but rather about the prospects for peace. A similar mistake is made in regard to Nietzsche's writings. They are iconoclastic, yes, but also became increasingly palliative as he undertook his later books. The conclusion of *Steppenwolf* doesn't echo the reconciliation of *Demian*; Haller's salvation, if you want to call it that, is discovered in the midst of turmoil. On a certain level, Haller completely fails to live happily in the Magic Theatre of his subconscious: he has random orgies, gets high, murders people, and flirts with suicide constantly. In the end, he plunges a knife into the only person he has ever loved—a woman named Hermine (the feminine form of Herman, as in "Hermann Hesse"), who most commentators agree is but a version of Harry himself, the only person he has ever *truly* loved.

It becomes clear—or as clear as it can be—that most of the book has been a dream: the violence, the irresponsibility, even the existential crisis is a product of Haller's mind. This makes it no less real but rather casts doubt on the distinction between illusion and one's waking hours. Haller's dream of the Magic Theatre is so vivid, so affecting that it overshadows what most people call "the real world." His regret, expressed in the closing dream sequence of the book, is as real as anything gets; so too is the lesson Haller gleans from the whole ordeal. Hesse wrote in 1919, in a little-known essay titled "Zarathustra's Return," "If you . . . are in pain, if you are sick in body or soul, if you are afraid and have a foreboding of danger—why not, if only to amuse yourselves . . . try to put the question in a different way? Why not ask whether the source of your pain might be inside you yourselves? . . . Might it not be an amusing exercise for each one of you to examine what ails you and try to determine its source?" Perhaps the hardest part of the eternal return is to own up to the tortures that we create for ourselves and those we create for others. Owning up: to recollect, to regret, to be responsible, ultimately to forgive and love. "What makes me Zarathustra," Hesse contended, "is that I have come to know Zarathustra's destiny. That I have lived his life. Few men know their destiny. Few men live their lives. Learn to live your lives."

Some life lessons are hard-won. After killing Hermine, Haller is accosted by the characters of the Magic Theatre; he fully expects them to execute him for his crime. In fact, in a rare moment of single-mindedness, he relishes the idea of this seemingly ultimate punishment. But his judges have other ideas: Haller is condemned not to death but to life. "You are to live," they instruct Haller, "and learn to laugh." It seems so simple, but given the madhouse of Haller's mind, this was an infinitely harder task than committing suicide. Yet it was, he concludes, the sentence that many human beings eventually face.

Enough with the "pathos and death dealing," a judge commands. "It is time that you come to your senses." Haller clenches his teeth, and for good reason—his adult life has been consumed with pathos, death-dealing, and running from the simple sensations of living. But he does, after a moment of protest, not only accept but genuinely embrace the disasters of life. This is what Nietzsche calls the *"amor fati,"* the love of fate. In the final scene of *Steppenwolf,* Haller reflects that he "felt hollow, exhausted, ready to sleep for a whole year," but he had glimpsed something of the meaning of "life's game": "I would sample its tortures once more and shudder again at its senselessness. I would traverse not once more, but often, the hell of my inner being. One day I would be better at the game. One day I would learn how to laugh."

Laughter: that was the key to the *amor fati.* The tortures of life's game—even in a game that seems largely painless—would endure. Resisting or denying these tensions and strivings would only intensify their force. The point of life was not to "get a grip" but to loosen one's hold just enough to get a fleeting sense of release. "Some of us think that holding on makes us strong," Hesse remarked, "but sometimes it is letting go." Genuine laughter would be long in coming, but it would remain the goal.

Nietzsche explains that "when we dream about those who are long since forgotten or dead, it is a sign that we have undergone a radical transformation and that the ground on which we live has been completely dug up: then the dead rise up, and our antiquity becomes modernity." I rose and helped Carol to her feet, and we guided each other out of the mountains and into the high valley. We were traveling, once again, in step with the sheep, but this time I didn't mind. Nietzsche had such disdain for these animals; masters and predators loved them only because they were delicious. There was, however, something untamed about the beasts' movements, the remnants of some deeply buried inclination to climb and run. They were still, on some hidden level, wild, and I no longer wished to deny that. The river that bisected the valley and separated us from the animals grew wide and shallow, and we looked for a point to cross. I could have jumped, but I'd had quite enough of that for the day, so we just walked together through the swirling ankle-deep water toward our hiking companions. By the time we reached the beasts, my feet were numb and finally clean.

A small crowd had gathered at the opening of the glacial plain to welcome us back. We had inadvertently stepped into a yearly ritual in the Engadine. The sheep graze on one ridge of the Fex Valley until mid-August and then are herded across to the other side until winter sets in during late September. At the end of fall, their vacation is over and they travel back to the farms of their origin. The cycle is the same every year. Nine hundred and sixty-one: that was the head count, including the two of us. We stopped at the edge of the crowd; they were taking pictures and clapping—I kid you not—for the sheep. These half-domesticated animals had survived another stint in the mountains, so there was something to clap about. I'm sure I am just projecting, but the animals seemed genuinely happy, scampering the last dozen feet into a holding pen where their hooves would be checked and sick ones would receive a bit of care.

Jocose—that is the word for them, playful to the point of lawlessness. Their wool had been tagged with spray paint, and several of them shared the same color, but each one was singular and surprisingly independent. A ewe nipped at an onlooker who held a selfie stick. Two lambs bumped into each other in a way that could only be intentional. An adolescent, on the edge of sheephood, stood pensively in the corner of the pen, taking in the gathering spectacle. Another put her hooves on the top rail of the fence and demanded attention. And then there was the brown, shaggy wizened one who had escaped last year's shearing. His wool was long and matted, and he looked like a cross between a ram and a sheepdog. I couldn't see his eyes under the overgrowth, but he seemed to get around just fine. Maybe he would escape shearing again this year. Maybe not.

I'd never seen an actual shepherd before. As a child, I thought that a shepherd was someone who led his flock, like the Pied Piper from Jean-François Millet's *The Shepherd Returns*. In this case, all the fellow has to do is show up and the sheep follow him in docile procession. After reading Nietzsche as a young man, my perspective on the shepherd changed; he was the figure from Van Gogh's *Shepherd with a Flock of Sheep*: a man brandishing a stick over the heads of stupid beasts. Shepherd as sadist. In truth, the shepherds here were completely different. They didn't lead the herd (these sheep were not about to follow mindlessly), but they didn't beat the animals either.

The head shepherd was an elfish-looking man who, even with his traditional pointed cap, came up to my shoulder. He couldn't have been more than a hundred and twenty pounds. His body was sinewy and weathered—not unlike Hesse's—and his small barrel chest attached directly to slim thighs that terminated in a pair of sculpted calves. These were Wordsworth's calves, the muscles of a great walker. His lungs, I am sure, were even more impressive. Lungs on legs: this is all he was.

He'd helped a few wayward animals across the river, a ferryman of sorts, and now he strode among them, checking

hooves and ears as he went. Occasionally he would find an animal in need of help, and standing astride of it, leaning over the
animal's back, he would grab two handfuls of its wool and,
with a single jerk, upend the beast. After the treatment had
been performed, he would relinquish control and the sheep
would go on its way without resentment. It was hard work, but
the shepherd smiled through it all: merry, wide-eyed, with a
thin-lipped smirk. At the end of the morning he stepped out
of the pen, cracked a beer, and ate an enormous hunk of cheese.
There was absolutely nothing special about the man save for
his calves and his face, which simply glowed. At some point in
the previous hour Carol and I had tracked down the apple
strudel and found two beers of our own. I didn't understand
the enlightened shepherd, but I was, and remain, deeply interested. He walked down to the river with his cheese, took his
boots off, and plunged his feet into the rushing current.

I'd hiked through this country for many days as a young
man, and I must have crossed this river too, but not at the same
place. The water swept down the valley and disappeared. I
looked back to the paddock and caught sight of three sheep
chasing one another in circles, not unlike rabbits, bounding
toward each other and scampering away. I remembered the
symbol of the three hares, and for just a moment I felt the sooth-
ing, almost reassuring sense of their eternal return. The earliest instance of the three hares is dated to the fifth century. It
was found in the Mogoa Caves, also known as the Thousand
Buddha Grottoes, a network of Buddhist temples in the hills of
northern China, at the edge of the Gobi Desert. Here the three
hares meant many things: recovery, fertility, tranquility in
motion, endless return. But the Buddhist hieroglyph also had a
single meaning, simple and perplexing—a way of expressing

the verb *to be*. Existence itself. Or maybe this is all wrong—
still too serious and complex—and the "three hares" are just
one's rising laughter when watching animals run in circles.

In the last years of Nietzsche's life he signed his letters
"Dionysus," but in a letter written to Cosima Wagner on the
day of his mental collapse in Turin, he wrote, "I am Buddha."
At some point in his life it might have even been true—
Nietzsche might have experienced something of enlightenment. His later writing may be the repeated, often frenzied
attempt to express it. Hesse, however, explains that "words
do not express thoughts very well. They always become a
little different immediately after they are expressed. A little
distorted. A little foolish." Words reify something experienced in motion, attempting to capture the forever unruly.

Hesse was a Nietzschean but also a mystic, an orientation
that granted him an insight that evades most of us. Indeed, I
suspect it escaped Nietzsche for much of his life. "Perhaps you
seek too much," Hesse suggests, "that as a result of your seeking
you cannot find." My entire life was—and, for the most part,
continues to be—about seeking and striving. I'm no Buddha,
but it is still possible, even for men like me, to catch sight of him
occasionally in others. I watched the shepherd walk upriver to
assume his ferryman post at the water's edge. Whom was he
waiting for? Closing his eyes, he tipped his head back toward
the sun and slowly chewed his last bite of cheese. He smiled
peacefully, graciously. I tried it, closed my eyes, but saw only
more words. Good words, but still words: "One never reaches
home, but wherever friendly paths intersect the whole world
looks like home for a time." Carol reached over with her fork,
stabbed a last piece of strudel, and placed it gently in my mouth.

"I miss Becca," I said. Carol nodded and kissed me lightly. We got up from the table where we'd eaten our snack, and we left the sheep and Siddhartha behind.

DAYS BEFORE HIS COLLAPSE, Nietzsche wrote, "I have often asked myself whether I am not more heavily obligated to the hardest years of my life than to any others." By the end, he seems to suggest, it is precisely these years that gave him the chance to explore what he took to be life's driving imperative. It's deceptively simple: "Become who you are."

This is the command Nietzsche gives his readers in *Thus Spoke Zarathustra* and what serves as the motivating force in *Ecce Homo*. What does it mean to search for ourselves? For most of my life I'd thought that my authentic self was something "out there," something beyond the quotidian, something on a mountain high in the Alps. I preferred to think of myself as existing somewhere else, in an unperturbed realm of transcendence. I was always secretly looking for this, resenting any person who might get in my way.

On some level, I probably got a divorce and married Carol because I thought it would allow me to find my true self, the permanent and enduring essence that underlies my personality. I remember too vividly an argument with my ex-wife that terminated with three words that I screamed before slamming our front door: "Let. Me. Be!" I now know what I actually meant: "Get out of my way." Let me find my immutable essence. Unfortunately, there is no such thing as an immutable essence, at least not in my world. And so I left, but I never found what I was looking for, not even with Carol and Becca. I found something else.

As it turns out, to "become who you are" is not about finding a "who" you have always been looking for. It is not about separating "you" off from everything else. And it is not about existing as you truly "are" for all time. The self does not lie passively in wait for us to discover it. Selfhood is made in the active, ongoing process, in the German verb *werden*, "to become." The enduring nature of being human is to turn into something else, which should not be confused with going somewhere else. This may come as a great disappointment to one who goes in search of the self. *What* one is, essentially, is this active transformation, nothing more, nothing less. This is not a grand wisdom quest or hero's journey, and it doesn't require one to escape to the mountains. No mountain is high enough. Just a bit of cheese and any fast-moving river will suffice.

"Become what you are": it has been described as "the most haunting of Nietzsche's haunting aphorisms." It expresses an abiding paradox at the core of human selfhood: either you are who you are already, or you become someone other than who you are. In the first case, becoming oneself seems superfluous or impossible. In the second, becoming oneself seems to wash away any last vestige of identity. For a person like me, who is used to thinking in straight lines that extend from one moment to the next in a semi-continuous fashion, this paradox is utterly infuriating. This frustration might be warranted, but I think Nietzsche and Hesse were encouraging us to venture beyond the straight and narrow: after all, the root of *werden* means "to bend, to wind, to turn into." It gives us *versus, ver-*

dict, and *vortex*. In becoming what one is, a person turns back, into, gathers something of the past, and carries it forward. It is genealogy compressed under high pressure. The present, as such, is but a placeholder where the past and future meet, a fleeting moment where becoming takes place.

When hikers bend into a mountain, there is a moment when they are neither ascending nor descending, but just on the verge. Everything happens so quickly at the pivot that capturing it is wholly impossible. In self-overcoming, one is on to the next moment before one knows what is happening. But something, regardless of one's ignorance, does in fact happen. Life continues to return. Human existence does not proceed from hell to purgatory to salvation—or if it does, it does so repeatedly, and its epicycles are so tight and short that you never fully arrive.

Nietzsche gestures toward the slipperiness of self-overcoming in *Schopenhauer as Educator*: "you are *not* really all that which you do, think, and desire now." And again, more dramatically, in *Ecce Homo*: "To become what one is, one must not have the faintest idea of what one is." I've never fully understood this point, but the moments where I've come closest are strange, uncanny, disruptive ones: hiking with Carol and the sheep in Val Fex, or watching our daughter dance on a hill of wildflowers, or getting lost for the first time when I was nineteen and again when I was thirty-six. Nietzsche's point may be that the process of self-discovery requires an undoing of the self-knowledge that you assume you already have. Becoming is the ongoing process of losing and finding yourself.

AS WE APPROACHED THE HOTEL, we heard children laughing through the trees. They were playing hide-and-seek in a field below the Waldhaus. Becca saw us coming from across the playground, said goodbye to her new friends, and came sprinting. I leaned down, grabbing her mid-stride, and hoisted her onto my hip. "Papa," she said breathing deeply, "you smell."

We both chuckled, and I carried her back to the room. On the way, with her face close to mine, she rubbed the back of my head and mindlessly played with my left earlobe. It was still sore. I held Carol's hand, and the Waldhaus came into view. "I want to walk," Becca whispered. I lowered her to the ground, and we watched her scamper up the hill, almost out of sight. We chased her for a minute—just for sport—and then let her go. She would wait for us at the top. By now she could find her own way to our room.

When Carol and I reached the Bellavista, the door was open. All was quiet. Becca was still playing hide-and-seek. We went in and wondered aloud, "Where could Becca be?" Still silence. The door to the balcony, which we'd locked before leaving, was ajar. Three stories up, the joy of the Bellavista was supposedly its elevation.

I opened the porch door. She wasn't hiding. There she sat, spellbound, on the polished concrete floor, looking westward as the sun set over Lake Sils, over the Maloja Pass, into Italy. This was the point to which everything led, the point from which everything flowed.

"Papa, can we go there?" Becca asked, pointing at the road that ran along the lake and bent into the fading light.

"Maybe next time, my love."

That was the way to Turin.

EPILOGUE:
MORGANSTREICH

*Repetition. It is an excellent thing to express a thing
consecutively in two ways, and thus provide it with a right
and a left foot. Truth can stand indeed on one leg, but
with two she will walk and complete her journey.*

—Friedrich Nietzsche,
The Wanderer and His Shadow, 1880

I T WAS FIVE MONTHS AFTER OUR RETURN FROM THE
Waldhaus. Our acclimation to normal life had been almost
seamless. A new preschool was happily attended. Syllabi were
dutifully written. Conferences were studiously organized.
Bathrooms were meticulously cleaned. Groceries were purchased and eaten. A cat was acquired. All this could have
been experienced passively enough—and I am sure some of it
was—but our last day in the Val Fex had cast shadow and light

over life for many weeks. On good days, it still does. I try to remember the shepherd-ferryman, to eat cheese between meals, and to do my best to become rather than to obsessively seek and control.

Modern life, however, is not entirely amenable to becoming who one is; it is designed to distract and deaden in all the ways that Nietzsche suggests. In the fall, after our return, I began to feel, once again, the Steppenwolf prowling at night. To see the sacred in the prosaic—this might be the objective of life, but I continued to miss the point. I went back on my little pink pills, but they didn't work exactly as they had earlier, and I still had dreams, most of them of the busy anonymous streets of Basel. I was usually sitting on the steps of the BIS, the banking capital of the world, with a box of marbles, watching people waste what is most valuable. And I was in their midst, part of the flow, trying to make something out of nothing. "You must find your dream," Hesse instructs, "but no dream lasts forever, each dream is followed by another, and one should not cling to any particular dream." I usually woke up, snuggled into Carol to reassure myself that this too would pass, or, on very bad nights, descended to the kitchen for a beer. I longed for another trip to Switzerland, if only to let Basel redeem itself.

MORGANSTREICH, OR "MORNING FLASH," comes in the dead of night. At 4:00 a.m. on a frigid March morning in the oldest section of Nietzsche's intellectual birthplace, a lantern is lit by a nameless figure. Another fire appears at a darkened doorway, and then another: thousands of small flames flicker against the walls of a city that usually gleams with the cold, anesthetic light of a million fluorescent bulbs. Then, in the firelight, the drumming begins—carnal, earth-pounding—rousing even the most committed sleepwalker. This has been happening in Basel every winter for nearly a thousand years.

I'd heard about the festival in my youth. When I read Nietzsche's letters for the first time, he'd mentioned that while working at the University of Basel he'd skip town to avoid the noise that would, for a raucous week, take hold of the frigid city. *Possess* is really more like it. Nietzsche was a young man when he fled *Morganstreich*. He was still seeking solace in the refined climes of Wagner and high art. The beating of the drums made his tender head hurt. I'd always thought he might have relished the festival a bit more had he joined the procession later in life, after he distanced himself from the pretenses of culture and more fully embraced his identity as Dionysus, as when he admits in *Ecce Homo*: "I am a disciple of the philosopher Dionysus; I would rather be a satyr than a saint."

In the fall of 1888, Nietzsche wrote nine poems under the pen name Dionysus. They are among his final pieces of writing. These "Dionysian Dithyrambs" are rarely read and even more rarely regarded as philosophically significant. They constitute the last burst of light before the darkness overtook Nietzsche in his final decade of life. They suit the spirit of *Morganstreich*:

> *This flame with a white-grey belly*
> *Flickers its greedy tongue into the cold beyond,*
> *Bends its neck towards ever purer heights—*
> *A raised serpent of impatience:*

This signal I placed before me.
My soul is this flame,
Insatiable for new expanses
To blaze upward, upward in silent passion.

The poem is called "Das Feuerzeichen," literally "the fire signal," the sort of beacons that are carried down the streets of Basel in the hours before first light. For a brief span in an otherwise boring year, the city is consumed by fire and snakes. These symbols of libido, power, and the earth appealed to this European Dionysus as he slipped toward the grave.

In his early years, Nietzsche mostly eschewed the throbbing, intoxicating mass of life—opting instead for the thin air of intellectual heights—but at least intellectually, he acknowledged its creative possibilities. In *The Birth of Tragedy*, he writes: "Either through the influence of the narcotic drink, of which the hymns of all aboriginal humans and peoples speak, or with the invigorating springtime's awakening that fills all nature with passion, these Dionysian impulses find their source, and as they grow in intensity everything subjective vanishes into complete loss of self-recognition."

The young Nietzsche acknowledged that there was something tragic about a refusal to give Dionysus his due. There are, however, some people—Nietzsche himself was often one of them—who from either "lack of experience or thick-headedness" turn away from the exhausting chaos of revelry for the sake of some semblance of mental health, "but of course these poor people have no idea how corpse-like and ghostly their so-called 'health' looks when the glowing life of the Dionysian swarm buzzes past them." There is something beautiful, indeed sacred, about the "loss of self-recognition" that the god of wine and dance grants. Nietzsche knew this but was rarely in a position to indulge in the ecstatic rapture that might be experienced with others. He chose austerity, isolation, and self-discipline until it thoroughly broke him. Only at the point of collapse did he begin to bellow like a man possessed.

AS THE FESTIVAL BEGINS, Basel is largely as I remember it: dull, routine. A few street vendors begin to gather, selling cheap masquerade costumes, but it looks, on the whole, like just another day of mediocrity. But as night falls, it's clear that ordinary days can pass into something else. For one night, revelers exchange their everyday masks, or cultural personas, for pointedly ghoulish ones, the kind that can't be ignored. Trickery, which is disavowed in daily life, is made shockingly apparent, and anonymity is assumed and pointedly enforced. It is rude, even forbidden, to ask others who they really are. As evening approaches, the superficiality of the city slowly disappears—everything seems to get deeper, darker, illusory, but also more honest. Before night even falls, individuals laugh and howl and make love as individuals—that is to say, exactly as they please.

People drink a bottle of wine, and then a pot of coffee, and then another bottle of wine—the propaedeutic for any Bacchic frenzy. The streets are filled with masks. Processions of drumming elves make their way toward a sound that splits the night: a pan flute, ethereal, plays above the beat. The musician is a horned beast—half-man, half-goat who carries its fellow carousers away into the panicked night.

Dionysus's adopted father, Silenus, played one of these flutes. Forever lighthearted, the satyr frolicked drunkenly through the forest of Greek mythology. He was enigmatic, uncatchable. When Midas tried to pin him down, to wrest from him the meaning of life, the little imp rebelled: the key to life is never to have been born, or if you are born, to die as quickly as possible. Live and die as quickly as possible. I've spent most of my adult life fixated on Silenus's nihilistic suggestion, ignoring what was most obvious about the creature, namely that he represented fertility and rebirth. Die as soon as you can—so that you can come to life again and again, like a morning flash, or spring after a brutal winter. There is another way to interpret the *Übermensch* that has little to do with perfectionism and self-stylizing: Nietzsche would like us to die, to get out of the way, to get out of our own way, so something else can take our place. So that we can become what we are.

The entire festival is in honor of death—to either appease it or become it—but ultimately for the sake of creation—or, better, re-creation. This is the wisdom of Silenus and why the satyr was chosen as Dionysus's guardian. Dionysus was twice-born, or, more dramatically, reborn. He died as quickly as possible, only to rise again. By some accounts he was the offspring of an illicit affair between Zeus and the goddess of the underworld, Persephone. Hera, Zeus's wife, discovered the adultery. Flying into a rage, she convinced the Titans, a family of primordial giants, to hunt the child down, dismember him, and cannibalize him. The only thing left when they were finished was the boy's heart. But Dionysus would live on.

When the Titans devoured him, Dionysus's body was

ground up, ingested, and digested by ancient giants. After Zeus found out about this act of revenge, he brought his son back to life and obliterated the Titans in a storm of lightning bolts. Nothing remained of the giants, just a wet soot: titanic and earthly, but with a hint, a mere fragrance, of something divine. It is a haunting admixture: the shame of ingratitude, tempered with the faint possibility of creativity and redemption. According to Orphic myth, Zeus combined this soot with clay to fashion small imperfect figures—humans. "Our body is Dionysian," the neo-Platonic philosopher Olympiodorus explains, "we are part of him, since we sprang from the soot of the Titans who ate of his flesh."

Eventually time lapses and the night recedes. The parade passes away and the sun rises. All great festivals are based on a cycle of death and rebirth. It doesn't matter where they're celebrated—Easter, Halloween, Ramadan, Diwali, Saturnalia, *Morganstreich*—they all have a similar flavor. Things must suffer, go dark, perish before they live again. This is not an escape or respite from life but rather its realization: in the end, to burn up and out, as Zarathustra does, "like a morning sun that comes out of dark mountains."

TIME LINE OF NIETZSCHE'S LIFE AND WRITINGS

1844

OCTOBER 15. Friedrich Wilhelm Nietzsche born to Karl Ludwig and Franziska Nietzsche.

1849

JULY. Nietzsche's father dies.

1858

Nietzsche begins school at Pforta.

1867

OCTOBER. Nietzsche enlists in an artillery regiment in Naumburg.

1868

OCTOBER. Nietzsche is discharged from the army.

1869

JANUARY. Nietzsche is appointed as professor at Basel University.
MAY. First meeting with Richard Wagner at Tribschen.

1872

JANUARY. Nietzsche applies for chair of philosophy at Basel.
NOVEMBER. Publication of *The Birth of Tragedy*.

1873
NOVEMBER. Essay on history (*Untimely Meditation* II).

1874
MARCH–SEPTEMBER. Works on *Schopenhauer as Educator* (*Untimely Meditation* III).

1876
FEBRUARY. Nietzsche stops teaching at university.
JULY. Nietzsche visits Wagner's Bayreuth Festival.
AUGUST. Begins work on *Human, All Too Human*.
OCTOBER. Paul Rée and Nietzsche stay in Sorrento with Malwida von Meysenbug. Nietzsche breaks with Wagner.
NOVEMBER. Nietzsche's final meeting with Wagner in Sorrento.

1878
JANUARY. *Human, All Too Human* sent to publisher.
AUGUST. Nietzsche falls ill.

1879
JUNE. Nietzsche travels to St. Moritz, near Sils-Maria.

1880
JANUARY–NOVEMBER. Nietzsche works on *The Dawn of Day*.

1881
JULY. Nietzsche travels to Sils-Maria.
AUGUST. Nietzsche begins to work on *Thus Spoke Zarathustra* and the "eternal return."
DECEMBER. Works on *The Gay Science*.

1882
MARCH. Fourth book draft completed for *The Gay Science*.
MAY. Nietzsche meets Lou Salomé in Rome.
AUGUST. Salomé comes to Tautenburg. *The Gay Science* published.

SEPTEMBER. Lou goes with Rée. Nietzsche plans for the three of them to live together in Paris, which never happens.
OCTOBER. Lou, Rée, and Nietzsche stay in Leipzig together.
NOVEMBER. Lou and Rée leave Nietzsche.

1883

JANUARY. *Thus Spoke Zarathustra* Part I written.
FEBRUARY. Nietzsche learns of Wagner's death.
OCTOBER. Nietzsche settles in Nice for the winter.

1884

JANUARY. *Zarathustra* Part II finished. Breach with Elisabeth, Nietzsche's sister.
JULY. Nietzsche to Sils-Maria to work on *Zarathustra* Part III.
DECEMBER. Nietzsche works on *Zarathustra* Part IV.

1885

MAY. Elisabeth marries Bernhard Förster, a reputed anti-Semite.
JUNE. Nietzsche begins *Beyond Good and Evil*.

1886

JANUARY. Nietzsche completes *Beyond Good and Evil*.
FEBRUARY. Elisabeth and Bernhard leave for Paraguay.
JUNE. Nietzsche goes to Sils-Maria. Begins to write *On the Genealogy of Morals*.

1887

NOVEMBER. *On the Genealogy of Morals* published.

1888

APRIL. Nietzsche moves to Turin.
JUNE. Leaves for Sils-Maria. Begins *Twilight of the Idols*.
SEPTEMBER. Begins work on *The Antichrist*.
OCTOBER. Begins to write *Ecce Homo*.

1889

JANUARY. Nietzsche collapses in the street in Turin.

JUNE. Bernhard Förster commits suicide.

1889–1897

Nietzsche is under the care of his mother.

1893

SEPTEMBER. Elisabeth, Nietzsche's sister, returns from Paraguay.

1895

DECEMBER. Nietzsche's mother signs away rights to Nietzsche's work, opening the way for his sister to take control of his corpus.

1897

EASTER. Nietzsche's mother dies.

1900

AUGUST 25. Nietzsche dies in Weimar.

1901

NOVEMBER. Paul Rée dies in a fall outside Sils-Maria.

SELECTED BIBLIOGRAPHY AND SUGGESTED READINGS

WORKS BY FRIEDRICH NIETZSCHE

The Antichrist. Translated by Walter Kaufmann in *The Portable Nietzsche*, edited by Walter Kaufmann. New York: Viking Press, 1968.
Beyond Good and Evil. Translated by Walter Kaufmann. New York: Random House, 1966.
The Birth of Tragedy. Translated by Walter Kaufmann in *The Birth of Tragedy and The Case of Wagner.* New York: Random House, 1967.
The Case of Wagner. Translated by Walter Kaufmann in *The Birth of Tragedy and The Case of Wagner.* New York: Random House, 1967.
The Dawn of Day. Translated by John Kennedy. London: T.N. Foulis, 1911.

Ecce Homo: How One Becomes What One Is. Translated by Walter Kaufmann in *On the Genealogy of Morals and Ecce Homo.* New York: Random House, 1967.

The Gay Science, with a Prelude of Rhymes and an Appendix of Songs. Translated by Walter Kaufmann. New York: Random House, 1974.

Human, All Too Human: A Book for Free Spirits. Translated by R. J. Hollingdale. Cambridge, UK: Cambridge University Press, 1986.

Kritische Gesamtausgabe Briefwechsel. Edited by G. Colli and M. Montinari, 24 vols. in 4 parts. Berlin: Walter de Gruyter, 1975.

Nietzsche Contra Wagner. Translated by Walter Kaufmann in *The Portable Nietzsche*, edited by Walter Kaufmann. New York: Viking Press, 1968.

On the Genealogy of Morals. Translated by Walter Kaufmann and R. J. Hollingdale in *On the Genealogy of Morals and Ecce Homo.* New York: Random House, 1967.

Thus Spoke Zarathustra. Translated by Walter Kaufmann in *The Portable Nietzsche*, edited by Walter Kaufmann. New York: Viking Press, 1968.

Twilight of the Idols. Translated by Walter Kaufmann in *The Portable Nietzsche*, edited by Walter Kaufmann. New York: Viking Press, 1968.

SECONDARY AND RELATED LITERATURE

Adorno, Theodor, and Max Horkheimer. *Dialectic of Enlightenment: Philosophical Fragments,* 1947. Edited by G. S. Noerr. Translated by E. Jephcott. Stanford, CA: Stanford University Press, 2002.

Allison, David. *Reading the New Nietzsche.* Lanham, MD: Rowman & Littlefield, 2000.

Babich, Babette E. "Become the One You Are: On Commandments and Praise Among Friends." In *Nietzsche, Culture, and Education.* Edited by Thomas Hart. New York: Routledge, 2017.

———. *Nietzsche's Philosophy of Science.* Albany: State University of New York Press, 1994.

———. *Words in Blood, Like Flowers: Philosophy and Poetry, Music and Eros in Hölderlin, Nietzsche, and Heidegger.* Albany: State University of New York Press, 2006.

Basho, Matsuo. *The Narrow Road to the Deep North.* New York: Penguin Press, 1966.

Bataille, Georges. *On Nietzsche,* 1945. Translated by Bruce Boone. London: Athlone Press, 1992.

Benjamin, Walter. *Selected Writings.* Vol. 4. Cambridge, MA: Harvard University Press, 2003.

Bishop, Paul, and R. H. Stephenson. *Friedrich Nietzsche and Weimar Classicism*. Rochester, NY: Camden House, 2005.

Blond, Lewis. *Heidegger and Nietzsche: Overcoming Metaphysics*. London: Continuum, 2011.

Chamberlain, Lesley. *Nietzsche in Turin: An Intimate Biography*. New York: Picador, 1998.

Clark, Maudemarie. *Nietzsche on Truth and Philosophy*. Cambridge, UK: Cambridge University Press, 1990.

Cohen, Jonathan R. *Science, Culture, and Free Spirit: A Study of Nietzsche's "Human, All-Too-Human."* Amherst, NY: Humanity Books / Prometheus Books. 2010.

Conant, James. "Nietzsche's Perfectionism: A Reading of *Schopenhauer as Educator*." In *Nietzsche's Postmoralism*. Edited by Richard Schacht. New York: Cambridge University Press, 2001.

Conway, Daniel. *Nietzsche and the Political*. New York: Routledge, 1997.

———. *Nietzsche's Dangerous Game: Philosophy in the Twilight of the Idols*. New York: Cambridge University Press, 1997.

Danto, Arthur C. *Nietzsche as Philosopher: An Original Study*. New York: Columbia University Press, 1965.

Deleuze, Gilles. *Difference and Repetition*, 1968. Translated by Paul Patton. New York: Columbia University Press, 1995.

———. *Nietzsche and Philosophy*, 1962. Translated by Hugh Tomlinson. New York: Columbia University Press, 1983.

Derrida, Jacques. *Spurs: Nietzsche's Styles*. Translated by Barbara Harlow. Chicago: University of Chicago Press, 1979.

Dostoyevsky, Fyodor. *Notes from Underground*, 1864. Translated by Richard Pevear and Larissa Volokhonsky. New York: Vintage, 1993.

Fasini, Remo. "Qui Venne Nietzsche" in *The Waldhaus Sils-Maria: English Edition*. Sils-Maria: No date.

Fink, Eugen. *Nietzsche's Philosophy*, 1960. Translated by Goetz Richter. Aldershot, UK: Avebury Press, 2003.

Geuss, Raymond. *Morality, Culture and History: Essays on German Philosophy*. Cambridge, UK: Cambridge University Press, 1999.

Gilman, Sander L., ed. *Conversations with Nietzsche: A Life in the Words of His Contemporaries*. Translated by David J. Parent. New York: Oxford University Press, 1987.

Goebel, Eckart. *Beyond Discontent: Sublimation from Goethe to Lacan*. London: Bloomsbury, 2012.

Greif, Mark. *Against Everything*. New York: Pantheon, 2016.

Gros, Frederic. *A Philosophy of Walking*. New York: Verso, 2014.

Hatab, Lawrence J. *Nietzsche's Life Sentence: Coming to Terms with Eternal Recurrence.* London: Routledge, 2005.

———. *Nietzsche's "On the Genealogy of Morality,"* Cambridge, UK: Cambridge University Press, 2008.

Hayman, Ronald. *Nietzsche, a Critical Life.* New York: Oxford University Press, 1980.

Heidegger, Martin. *Nietzsche, Vol. I: The Will to Power as Art,* 1936–37. Translated by David F. Krell. New York: Harper & Row, 1979.

———. *Nietzsche, Vol. II: The Eternal Recurrence of the Same,* 1936–37. Translated by David F. Krell. San Francisco: Harper & Row, 1984.

———. *Nietzsche, Vol. III: Will to Power as Knowledge and as Metaphysics,* 1939. Translated by Joan Stambaugh and Frank Capuzzi. San Francisco: Harper & Row, 1986.

———. *Nietzsche, Vol. IV: Nihilism,* 1939. Translated by David F. Krell. New York: Harper & Row, 1982.

Hesse, Hermann. *Siddhartha.* Translated by Joachim Neugroschel. New York: Penguin, 1999.

———. *Steppenwolf.* Translated by Basil Creighton. New York: Picador, 1963.

Higgins, Kathleen Marie. *Comic Relief: Nietzsche's Gay Science.* Oxford, UK: Oxford University Press, 1999.

———. *Nietzsche's "Zarathustra."* Philadelphia: Temple University Press, 1987.

Hollingdale, R. J. *Nietzsche.* London and New York: Routledge and Kegan Paul, 1973.

Irigaray, Luce. *Marine Lover of Friedrich Nietzsche,* 1980. Translated by Gillian C. Gill. New York: Columbia University Press, 1991.

Jameson, F. *Late Marxism: Adorno, or, The Persistence of the Dialectic,* London; New York: Verso, 1990.

Janaway, Christopher. *Beyond Selflessness: Reading Nietzsche's Genealogy,* Oxford, UK: Oxford University Press, 2007.

Jaspers, Karl. *Nietzsche: An Introduction to the Understanding of His Philosophical Activity,* 1936. Translated by Charles F. Wallraff and Frederick J. Schmitz. South Bend, IN: Regentry/Gateway, 1979.

Jung, Carl G. *Nietzsche's "Zarathustra,"* 1934–39. Edited by James L. Jarrett. Princeton, NJ: Princeton University Press, 1988.

Kain, Philip J. *Nietzsche and the Horror of Existence.* Lanham, MD: Lexington Books, 2009.

Katsafanas, Paul. *Agency and the Foundations of Ethics: Nietzschean Constitutivism.* Oxford, UK: Oxford University Press, 2013.

Kaufmann, Walter. *Nietzsche: Philosopher, Psychologist, Antichrist.* Princeton, NJ: Princeton University Press, 1950.

Kennedy, J. M. *Nietzsche.* New York: Haskell House, 1974.

Klossowski, Pierre. *Nietzsche and the Vicious Circle,* 1969. London: Athlone Press, 1993.

Kofman, Sarah. *Nietzsche and Metaphor,* 1972. Edited and translated by Duncan Large. London: Athlone Press; Stanford, CA: Stanford University Press, 1993.

Köhler, Joachim. *Nietzsche and Wagner: A Lesson in Subjugation.* Translated by Ronald Taylor. New Haven: Yale University Press, 1998.

Krell, David Farrell. *Postponements: Women, Sensuality, and Death in Nietzsche.* Bloomington: Indiana University Press, 1986.

Krell, David Farrell, and Donald L. Bates. *The Good European: Nietzsche's Work Sites in Word and Image.* Chicago: University of Chicago Press, 1997.

Leiter, Brian. *Routledge Guidebook to Nietzsche on Morality.* London: Routledge, 2002.

Lemm, Vanessa. *Nietzsche's Animal Philosophy: Culture, Politics and the Animality of the Human Being.* New York: Fordham University Press, 2009.

Liebert, Georges. *Nietzsche and Music.* Translated by David Pellauer and Graham Parkes. Chicago: University of Chicago Press, 2004.

Löwith, Karl. *Nietzsche's Philosophy of the Eternal Recurrence of the Same,* 1956. Translated by J. Harvey Lomax, foreword by Bernd Magnus. Berkeley: University of California Press, 1997.

Mandel, Siegfried. *Nietzsche & the Jews.* New York: Prometheus Books, 1998.

Mann, Thomas. *Doctor Faustus.* Translated by John E. Woods. New York: Knopf, 1992.

Martin, Clancy. *Love and Lies.* New York: Farrar, Straus and Giroux, 2015.

Matthiessen, Peter. *The Snow Leopard.* New York: Vintage, 2003.

May, Simon. *Nietzsche's Ethics and his War on "Morality."* Oxford, UK: Oxford University Press, 2000.

———, ed. *Nietzsche's "On the Geneaology of Morality": A Critical Guide.* Cambridge, UK: Cambridge University Press, 2011.

Mencken, H. L. *The Philosophy of Friedrich Nietzsche,* 1908. New Brunswick (U.S.) and London (UK): Transaction Publishers, 1993.

Mileck, Joseph. *Hermann Hesse: Life and Art.* London: University of California Press, 1981.

Mishima, Yukio. *Confessions of a Mask.* Translated by Meredith Weatherby. New York: New Directions, 1959.

Nehamas, Alexander. *Nietzsche: Life as Literature.* Cambridge, MA: Harvard University Press, 1985.

Oliver, Kelly. *Womanizing Nietzsche: Philosophy's Relation to the "Feminine."* New York and London: Routledge, 1995.

Parkes, Graham. *Composing the Soul: Reaches of Nietzsche's Psychology.* Chicago and London: University of Chicago Press, 1994.

Pippin, Robert B. *Nietzsche, Psychology and First Philosophy.* Chicago: University of Chicago Press, 2011.

Ratner-Rosenhagen, Jennifer. *American Nietzsche: A History of an Icon and His Ideas.* Chicago: University of Chicago Press, 2011.

Rosen, Stanley. *The Mask of Enlightenment: Nietzsche's Zarathustra.* Cambridge, UK: Cambridge University Press, 1995.

Salomé, Lou. *Nietzsche,* 1894. Edited and translated by Siegfried Mandel. Redding Ridge, CT: Black Swan Books, 1988.

Schacht, Richard. *Making Sense of Nietzsche: Reflections Timely and Untimely.* Champaign: University of Illinois Press, 1995.

———. *Nietzsche.* London: Routledge and Kegan Paul, 1983.

Shapiro, Gary. *Nietzschean Narratives.* Bloomington: Indiana University Press, 1989.

Simmel, Georg. *Schopenhauer and Nietzsche,* 1907. Translated by Helmut Loiskandle, Deena Weinstein, and Michael Weinstein. Urbana and Chicago: University of Illinois Press, 1991.

Smith, Gary, ed. *Benjamin: Philosophy, Aesthetics, History.* Chicago: University of Chicago Press, 1989.

Solnit, Rebecca. *Wanderlust: A History of Walking.* New York: Penguin, 2000.

Solomon, Robert C. *Living with Nietzsche: What the Great "Immoralist" Has to Teach Us.* Oxford, UK: Oxford University Press, 2003.

Steiner, Rudolph. *Friedrich Nietzsche: Fighter for Freedom.* New York: Herman, 1960.

Young, Julian. *Friedrich Nietzsche: A Philosophical Biography.* Cambridge, UK: Cambridge University Press, 2010.

———. *Nietzsche's Philosophy of Art.* Cambridge, UK: Cambridge University Press, 1992.

———. *Nietzsche's Philosophy of Religion.* Cambridge, UK: Cambridge University Press, 2006.

ACKNOWLEDGMENTS

This is the companion book to *American Philosophy: A Love Story*. When *American Philosophy* was published in 2016, Mark Greif wrote of the book that "the weight of transcendent meaning and mysticism which gets transferred from divinity to companionate marriage here (as everywhere else in our world) seems a cruelly heavy burden upon intimate life." He's right. This observation—so incisive and disturbing—is one of the driving forces behind *Hiking with Nietzsche*.

I would like to thank Clancy Martin, who urged me to start writing and kept me on course. Initially we'd planned on writing this book together, and in many ways I wish we had. But Clancy, in an act of generosity and good guidance, suggested that I journey alone, or just with Carol and Becca. It was the right choice. But he remains one of the hidden players in the manuscript. Our discussions of fatherhood, love, companionship, and deception percolate through the book in ways that I continue to discover and wish to acknowledge. It had been a long time since I'd read Nietzsche. Clancy served as my reintroduction by proxy.

I wish to also thank Daniel Conway and Douglas Anderson. Without their support I would never have made the first trip to Switzerland, or become a philosopher, or finished college. They remain the most thoughtful teachers a student could hope to encounter. A host of other mentors and teachers joined them to guide me, first with *American Philosophy: A Love Story* and now with *Hiking with Nietzsche*: Jennifer Ratner-Rosenhagen, Megan Marshall, Philip Kitcher, Andre Dubus III, Patricia Meyer Spacks, Lydia Moland, Nathan Glazer, Mark Johnson, Chis Lydon, Mary McGrath, John Russon, Gordon Marino, Michael Raposa, Whitley Kaufman, and Victor Kestenbaum, among many others. I am indebted to James Conant's insights concerning Nietzsche's perfectionism (the challenge to lean into "the unattained and attainable self") and to Alexander Nehamas's reading of Nietzsche, especially his interpretation of the relationship between narrative, autobiography, and philosophy. Nehamas is quite right in saying that the imperative to "become what you are" is, in his words, "the most haunting of Nietzsche's haunting aphorisms." Julian Young's reading of Nietzsche's life was indispensable, as was Babette Babich's *Words in Blood, Like Flowers*.

I am grateful for the dear friends who support Carol, Becca, and me: Alice Frye, Scott Davidson and Ann de Saussure Davidson, Tess and Ken Pope, Amelia Wirts and Jose Mendoza, Susanne Sreedhar, Subrena and David Smith, Peter Aldinger (who read the manuscript through before the rest), Nick Pupik, Ji Park (who walked with Nietzsche and me years before the first trip to Switzerland), Emily Stowe, and Jen McWeeny. Marianna Alessandri read multiple versions of the book and made me aware of a phrase—"love's conditions"—that I'd never considered and will never forget. Another friend, Romel Sharma, also deserves special mention. Romel was my temporary travel companion on my first sojourn to Europe. After leaving Sils-Maria, he and I hiked through Italy and France for days on an absolute shoestring, and I think we were fortunate to make it home in one piece.

An expanding handful of editors have helped in reframing and honing my writing: Jean Tamarin, Alex Kafka, Peter Catapano, Alex Kingsbury, Sam Dresser, Jesse Barron, John Knight, Paul Jump, Ken Barton, and Phil Marino. I'd like to thank my agent, Markus Hoffmann, for supporting this project and helping me refine my writing and thinking. He has been a most astute reader of early drafts and has the uncanny ability to lead without leading. Carol Hay, of course, was the closest and most exacting reader of the book. Thank you.

When I was thirty-one, I went to the offices at Farrar, Straus and Giroux to talk to Ileene Smith about the initial proposal for *American Philosophy: A Love Story*. I was new enough to the publishing industry not to know how intimidated I should have been. At the end of the conversation she said she would "think about it" and discuss it with her colleagues. I am sure I would have let the project fade had she not called me back and encouraged me first to write *American Philosophy* and now this book on Nietzsche. I am profoundly grateful to Ileene and FSG for the opportunity to write these books and work myself out over their pages. I'd like to thank Jackson Howard, Rachel Weinick, and Maxine Bartow for their outstanding editorial support.

I wish to thank my mother, Becky Kaag, and my brother, Matt. I am not like Hermann Hesse in many respects, but I was, I know, a complete handful as a child, and they are largely responsible for seeing me into adulthood and not shipping me off to a caretaker. The growing brood of our extended family—Brian, Karen, Jeremy, James, Solomon, Flora, Allie, Matt, Carin, David, Talie—continues to remind me that life, happily, outpaces philosophy.

Carol and Becca, my companions on this trip and in all things: I want to thank you for loving me despite, and perhaps because of, the masks that I occasionally wear. I love you both more than I could ever express in words.

INDEX